This book is dedicated to the late Douglas Bunn,
whose vision, determination and flair created the
All England Jumping Course at Hickstead, and
to all those who helped make his dream a reality.

HICKSTEAD
HICKSTEAD
START

HICKSTEAD

A GOLDEN CELEBRATION

ALAN SMITH LOOKS BACK ON 50 YEARS OF THE ALL ENGLAND JUMPING COURSE

FOREWORD BY HRH THE DUKE OF EDINBURGH

Contents

2
Polistas

PRO

Foreword

By HRH The Duke of Edinburgh

I came into contact with Douglas Bunn while I was President of the International Equestrian Federation, which happened to coincide with his creation of Hickstead. The FEI is the authority for all international competitions and championships and the enforcement of its Rules and Regulations has always been a matter for negotiation with the organising committees of international and championship events. Douglas Bunn was inclined to want to have things his own way, and this led, on occasions, to quite keen negotiations, although, I have to say, if he could see a good reason for any objections to his proposals, he was usually prepared to accept it.

As a result of several visits to Hickstead, it was quite obvious to me that he was a 'visionary' with a single-minded dedication to show jumping and with a burning ambition to develop Hickstead into the national equestrian centre. Its success now stands as his monument.

During one of my visits to Hickstead, I noticed several, what might be described as, 'outer rings'. I asked Douglas how they were used. Apart from minor jumping events and showing classes, he explained that he made them available to a local equestrian club for jumping competitions. The members paid a membership fee, part of which went in rent, and an entry fee for each competition, and they organised the whole thing themselves. This struck me as a splendid idea, which I thought could be made to work on Smith's Lawn at Windsor on the space on the other side of the road from the polo grounds. I mentioned the idea to Mike Ansell, who was then the guiding spirit of all equestrian disciplines in the country and a member of the FEI Bureau. He instantly approved, and within months had found Lt.Col. Frank Beale, and persuaded him to run it. The Windsor Park Equestrian Club was formed in 1970, and proved to be an instant success. It now has some 1,000 members and organises competitions over two days every month through the summer. Apart from show jumping, and dressage classes, there is also a thriving carriage driving section. I mention this because it is a direct legacy of Douglas Bunn's enthusiasm and imagination.

Philip

Introduction

By Alan Smith

This book was originally planned both as a celebration of the first 50 years of the All England Jumping Course at Hickstead, Sussex, and as a surprise gift to its founder, Douglas Bunn, from his family. Sadly, following Douglas's death in 2009, a few days before the British Jumping Derby Meeting, it is now a testimonial to what he achieved during that half-century.

I was delighted when asked if I would write it, as Hickstead played an enormous part in my own career as *The Daily Telegraph's* equestrian correspondent, which began in 1960, the year, of course, in which Hickstead opened its gates, and lasted until my retirement in December 2008: a retirement which has given me the time to write it. Fifty years is far too long a period for me to be able to recount every incident, but I hope that I have covered the important moments in the story, so far, of a showground that shaped British show jumping when the sport most needed it, and continues to do so. I know that, in Douglas's family, it remains in safe hands.

The willing response from everyone I have asked to help in the project, such as Bill Steinkraus's eloquent tribute to Douglas's forethought and his hospitality; David Broome's appreciation of what Douglas and Hickstead meant to him and to the sport; the piece written by Jane Kidd, with her insight into dressage at Hickstead, and Margaret Shaw's review of showing classes; and the many tributes by riders and officials, are, I think, ample testament of the regard and esteem in which Douglas was held, and of the success of his dream.

I would like to thank my colleagues, Max Ammann (*The FEI Championships*), Sue Clarke (*Forgie, the story of Pennwood Forge Mill*), Michael Clayton and Dick Tracey (*Hickstead, the first 12 years*), Judith Draper (*Guinness Book of Show Jumping*), Genevieve Murphy (*Jump-Off*, David Broome's biography) and Michael Slavin (*Irish Show Jumping Legends*) who have given me permission to use excerpts or statistics from their own books. Also thanks to those who helped me find the photographs that have illustrated the book: in particular Trevor Meeks and the *Horse and Hound* picture desk, Max Ammann and the FEI's picture library, Clive Thompson of CT Print, and David P. Barker of Waugh & Co., executors of my late friend, Leslie Lane. And finally my thanks to Peter Jeffery, Hickstead's long-serving press officer, to Paul Harding, whose brilliant design and production has made this book what it is, to Barbara Cooper, whose idea it was to produce it ourselves, and Judith Draper, for her meticulous editing—far beyond what a newspaperman is used to.

Alan Smith and his faithful dog, Branwen.

Douglas's Dream

'Douglas Bunn was undoubtedly the greatest innovator in British show jumping in post-war years. He succeeded in creating his personal vision virtually on his doorstep and he made the horse world come to him in his native Sussex.' – MICHAEL CLAYTON

Douglas Bunn had a dream. He wanted to create in England a showcase for competitions that would display the skilful horsemanship, the variety of obstacles and the sheer public-appealing excitement that he had seen at horse shows in Europe. And he wanted to do it in style: to have what he described as a 'Glyndebourne of show jumping'.

It was to be an expensive dream, once or twice verging on a financial nightmare, and demanded a lifelong commitment to overseeing it. But, during the first 50 years of the All England Jumping Course at Hickstead, he did achieve it; despite his sad death in 2009 his family have collectively ensured that the dream lives on.

Douglas was born on February 29, 1928, and brought up on the farm at Selsey, in West Sussex, to which his parents, George and Alice, had moved from London. From his infancy he was surrounded by ponies and horses and it was soon clear that they were to play a huge part in his life. He was put on a pony, Billy Boy, at the age of four, and when it deposited him through a sheet of glass, he merely asked to be put back on. That was the leitmotif for his entire life—problems were there to be solved, not given in to.

He showed a precocious riding talent to go with his determination, and had the good fortune to live close to Bill Gardner, whose son Phil was champion junior show-jumping rider in the mid-1930s. In 1937, when Phil turned 16 and was too old to ride in junior competitions, George Bunn asked Gardner senior if he would like 10-year-old Douglas to take over.

Douglas recalled, in Michael Clayton and Dick Tracey's book *Hickstead: the first twelve years*: 'Bill Gardner agreed and I shall always remember my first ride for him, at Odiham, Hampshire, on August Bank Holiday Monday, 1938. I was riding probably the best 13.2 hands pony in England. His name was Joby, and the only problem was that I couldn't ride one side of him.'

But he soon learned how to, and with Joby and Gardner's other top-class ponies the young Douglas enjoyed a summer of tremendous success. It was a run that continued during 1939 until the outbreak of the Second World War, when almost all of the 40 or so horses on the farm were bought for the Army, to go to the Middle East. Only two horses and two ponies were left behind, and most of the pasture was ploughed up to grow food. Douglas, who was being educated at Chichester High School, was not to ride competitively again until 1944.

His partnership with Bill Gardner resumed, and in 1945 Douglas's father bought, unseen and from an advertisement in *Horse and Hound* a horse, Rahin, belonging to Jed O'Dwyer, a member of the Irish team which in the 1930s was among the best in the world. He paid £500, and the horse was sent by train to Chichester, where he arrived on V.E. Day—when the country was celebrating Victory in Europe. He was met by Douglas's brother George, who took three hours to walk him back to Selsey, where the horse promptly lay down in a state of exhaustion.

First impressions of the Irish thoroughbred were not favourable, but they were wrong—though his well-used forelegs always needed careful handling—and Douglas later said that 'Rahin was the horse who taught me how to ride'. For the next four seasons they were winning one competition after another, and at the Victory Show in London's White City Stadium in September 1946, they finished second to Harry Llewellyn on Kilgeddin, who was to be in Britain's bronze medal team, ridden by Henry Nicoll, with Llewellyn himself on Foxhunter, in the London Olympic Games in 1948.

Douglas always maintained that for show jumpers to win at the top level in those days they had to be as well trained as dressage horses. With slats still being used on top of poles, and penalties awarded for touches as well as knockdowns, they had to be ultra-precise. Although he was to be, as he showed at Hickstead, a great innovator, he

PAGE 8: Douglas Bunn in the garden of Hickstead Place with the globular sundial, a 70th birthday present from his family and friends

had considerable respect for the way horses were then being ridden. He said: 'Nowadays you see people winning Grands Prix, at, say, Hickstead, Aachen and Rome, with rounds which are terribly hit-or-miss.'

During and just after the war Douglas was up at Trinity College, Cambridge, studying law, with a 20-month interruption in 1946 when he was called up for National Service. His studies were also interrupted, on a more frequent basis, by his riding, though a casual observer might not have noticed, for while he rode as Douglas Bunn his studies were conducted using the family name, Honeybunn. His tutor at Trinity told him he could not have a pupil masquerading under two names and he must choose one surname for both. He chose Bunn, the name which has since reverberated around, and often beyond, the equestrian world.

In 1952 he married his first wife, of three, Roseymee, with whom he had three children, Claudia, Lavinia and Theresa. He was called to the Bar at Lincoln's Inn in 1953, where he practised as a barrister until 1959. His life then was so hectic he would sometimes appear in court wearing breeches beneath his gown and striped trousers, ready to dash off to a show. Most importantly, he had added another dimension to an already crowded itinerary with the creation, at Selsey, of the first of the caravan parks—appropriately the White Horse Caravan Park—which were to finance his life, and Hickstead, in the ensuing years.

He made his British team début in Geneva in 1957, and by 1959 it was clear that there was not enough time to continue his career in law. That was the year when he bought Hickstead Place, a manor house dating back in parts to the 13th century, which had been purchased in 1542 by Richard Stapley and been in the hands of his descendants until Douglas bought it. He had always intended that his showground should be in Sussex, and the location was perfect for what he wanted, being alongside the A23, the main London-to-Brighton road, with Gatwick airport just a short drive away. Only 30 acres went with the house, but purchase of an adjacent farm later took that to 100 acres. The setting for the showpiece he was about to create was in place.

The winter of 1959-60 was one of intense activity as Douglas, with the help of a local forestry worker, Ernie Fish, who was to become the show manager during its formative years, measured out and started to set up what was to become the International Arena. Although the Derby Bank was added a year later, many of the other permanent obstacles were built then: the water jump and double of water ditches, the Irish Bank, the table,

Douglas Bunn leading the field at a meet of the Mid-Surrey Farmers' Draghounds. Sue Bunn is on the right, just behind the grey horse.

now called the Road Jump, and, perhaps the most difficult obstacle of all, the Devil's Dyke.

It was during his early years of jumping abroad that Douglas had conceived the idea of creating a showground that, as well as providing spectacular entertainment for the public, would give British riders the chance to ride over fences of the sort they would encounter at the top overseas shows, unlike what he described as the 'utterly pathetic' courses that were the norm at British shows in those days.

Sue, initially his groom but who in 1960 became Douglas's second wife, and with whom he had three more children, Edward, Lizzie and John, went with him to many continental shows. She remembers: 'It used to frustrate him that when we went on a team abroad we used to have to start training when we got there. The horses used to look horrified at banks, and ditches, and water ditches, and Douglas said that "One day I am going to build something that will allow us to train in England before we go across to the continent." So everywhere we went I used to have to have a tape-measure with me, and a little book and pencil. At the shows he'd say "Just go and measure that bank, or that ditch", and the other riders used to think "Douglas is very thorough, getting his missus to measure all the fences." Little did they know it was all going in the little black book to come back here.'

Although Douglas had had well-publicised differences of opinion, especially in connection with related distances between fences, with Jack Talbot-Ponsonby, who at that time was Britain's premier course-designer—even walking out of the 1967 Horse of the Year Show in protest, when he said one would have to 'pull a horse's back teeth out' to get round one such course—the two remained firm friends until Jack died, aged just 62, in 1969. Jack and Colonel Sir Mike Ansell, who drew up a blueprint for British show jumping while in a prisoner-of-war camp, and then ruled the sport, firmly but beneficially, after the war, were Douglas's two principal mentors.

It was to Jack Talbot-Ponsonby that Douglas took his early designs for the Hickstead Arena in 1959 for hours of discussion about the general lay-out and the design and construction of the obstacles. And it was Jack T-P, as he was universally known, who suggested to Douglas that he should get in touch with Pamela Carruthers, an international show jumper just before and after the war, who was beginning her career as a course designer.

In May 1960 the All England Jumping Course opened its doors—on possibly the least-auspicious weekend of the entire summer. The first day, a Friday, clashed with the televised wedding of Princess Margaret and Anthony Armstrong-Jones, and the second with the F.A. Cup Final at Wembley. If spectators were in short supply, just a couple of weeks before the show it looked as though there might be very little for those who did go to watch anyway. When the initial entries closed, there was just one, Bill Reece from Devon, and Cubhunter.

Douglas, in *Hickstead: the first twelve years*, remembered that day: 'I couldn't believe it. When the entries closed I set to, phoning all my friends in the show-jumping world and asking them: "Why aren't you entering?" They replied: "Well, we'd like to see what happens first." So I said to them: "Everyone has been claiming for years that what we need in this country is a permanent show-jumping arena. Now I've built one, and I've got one entry. If you don't come, there's no horse show; that'll be the end of it." '

When the time came they had about 30 riders and a handful of spectators, in cars parked almost wherever they wanted round the perimeter of the vast arena. I well remember the Press Centre—a tent with a telephone nailed to an adjacent tree—and the Press Stand—a few bales of hay. But those who were there had their money's-worth.

As Douglas recalled: 'The first six horses in the ring all failed to get round. They

OPPOSITE PAGE: Douglas Bunn with Her Majesty The Queen, patron of the Royal International Horse Show

Douglas Bunn, after graduating from Trinity College, Cambridge, in 1951

refused at almost anything. Then Sue Connolly, who was to have ridden Cubhunter, said she would get Tom Brake to ride the horse for the first time over this new course. I'm convinced that Tom's vast experience hunting in the West Country enabled him to get round. Tom got up on Cubhunter and just 'hunted' him round. He just rode him as if he was taking a young horse hunting. Later Judy Shepherd jumped the first clear round at Hickstead on Thou Swell.'

Douglas, who was joint-master of the Mid-Surrey Farmers' Draghounds from 1976 to 2000, and would often fly himself to Leicestershire to hunt with the Quorn, had the greatest respect for Tom Brake as a man who was as passionate about hunting as he was. Both Tom, whom he called 'The best in the West', and Judy became enthusiastic supporters of Hickstead.

Judy won the first two Hickstead Gold Medals, awarded to the rider who gained the most points on one horse, in 1964 and 1965, and met her husband-to-be, Australian event rider Brian Crago, there. The Australian and British eventers trained at Hickstead before the Rome Olympic Games in 1960—which the Australians won in dramatic style—and were among the first of so many riders and others who enjoyed Douglas's hospitality over the next half-century.

Bill Steinkraus, captain of the United States team and Mexico Olympic gold medal winner, has written in his own eloquent style of their frequent visits to Hickstead, and Peter Winton, former rider and now a show organiser in Kuala Lumpur, happily acknowledges his own debt: 'I first came to Hickstead in 1965 with the Australian team, and for me it was like paradise. I learned so much and established a really wonderful friendship with Douglas and his family. He said 'Come and stay at Hickstead' and that was one of the reasons I decided to leave Australia and come to Europe. I rode for him for some years, and even when I travelled around Europe Hickstead was my base.'

In that first season, Douglas had planned no fewer than six meetings, mostly of just three days each, and despite the problems of that first show, and the financial loss it made, he persevered, with gradually increased support from riders and the public as the All England Jumping Course became better known. For the riders, and for the press it must be added, those early shows were tremendous fun, almost all of them ending with a party—a tradition that Douglas maintained with style for the rest of his life.

Busy though he was with Hickstead, Douglas found time to go to other shows, sometimes flying himself to those in Europe, and none turned out to be more important to him than the Taunton Jumping Festival, run at her home by the Hon. Janet Kidd, who was to be a tower of strength at the AEJC for years to come. There Douglas met the chairman and promotion manager of W.D. & H.O. Wills, Bill Carter and Ken Cotell, who saw Hickstead's possibilities, and offered to sponsor the shows. It was a sporting partnership that lasted 20 years, and Douglas was adamant that without it Hickstead certainly would not have thrived as it did, and probably would not have been able to continue at all.

Their first sponsored show was at the end of the 1960 season, and it was at a debriefing session involving the four of them—Bunn, Mrs Kidd, Carter and Cotell—that autumn that two important decisions were reached. The first was to appoint Pamela Macgregor-Morris, esteemed equestrian correspondent of *The Times*, as the show's press officer; the second was to establish, as Douglas called it, 'a competition with an heroic quality. We should call it the British Jumping Derby.'

The story of how Douglas went to Hamburg on a bleak winter's day to measure their famous Derby Bank has become the stuff of legend. He had seen a newsreel film of the Hamburg Derby, and had to go and see the course for himself. He flew out on a sunny New Year's Eve, and arrived in a snowstorm. He had arranged to visit the course with

Douglas Bunn at the controls of his Cessna aeroplane

Following a riding accident, Douglas had to follow the Mid-Surrey Farmers' Draghounds meet at Hickstead on a somewhat safer conveyance.

the Hamburg officials, but they expected the snow to put him off. They did not know the man. With tape measure, a meat skewer to secure one end of it, and a notebook, he walked the course, noting in his book the dimensions of all the permanent obstacles.

When he was halfway round, the President of the show, other officials and the groundsman arrived, and Douglas said: 'I shall never forget the look on their faces. They were clearly thinking "This is the craziest Englishman you ever met".' They invited him to their New Year's Eve party, but he had to finish his measuring first. By the time he came to the Bank, the snow was six inches deep, which may be why, when it was built, Hickstead's Bank was six inches bigger than Hamburg's—though it was probably just that Douglas wanted it, like everything he did, to be bigger and better than anyone else's. Then he went to their New Year's Eve party.

The story of the Hickstead Bank continues in the section on the British Jumping Derby, but that of the first rider to come down it, Alison Westwood, deserves its place here: 'Hickstead decided the whole of my life. We went to the first-ever meeting, and enjoyed it so much we kept going. My mother bought Coady from Douglas Bunn and he was my first Grade A horse; he wasn't a winner but he was the most wonderful schoolmaster because he could jump anything correctly; never stopped; never had a drama. I knew I could go into the main ring in the big classes and not make a fool of myself. We came down the Bank first because I thought "It's the only thing he can't knock down. Here's a chance to get my name in the paper!" ' They came down the Bank without mishap, and Alison's name was in the papers often after her mother bought another horse from Douglas, The Maverick, on which, among many other competitions, she won the Derby twice, in 1968 and 1973, as well as the Queen Elizabeth II Cup in 1969 and silver and bronze European Championship medals.

Douglas was still competing, principally on Beethoven—whom he had bought at the

same time as The Maverick—and in 1962 won the Martini International Club's award as Horseman of the Year. He was also sometimes chef d'équipe of the British team, including at the World Championships in La Baule, 1970, when David Broome won the individual title on Beethoven. So it is not surprising that he felt the need to have a resident course-builder to carry some of the day-to-day pressure, and Pam Carruthers proved an inspired choice.

As a former international rider who had competed on the continent, she knew the sort of fences and courses that Douglas aspired to, but was comparatively new to course designing. Douglas, who by no means wanted to relinquish all control over the Hickstead courses, said, in *Hickstead: the first twelve years*: 'I had my own ideas about how I wanted the courses at Hickstead to be. If I had had anyone else but Pam Carruthers working with me I'm sure there would have been terrible rows. An established course builder would have said: 'Look, if you know better, you build the ruddy courses yourself.' I'm not saying, mind you, that poor old Pam hasn't had a hard time. There used to be a few tears on occasion and Pam obviously thought I was impossible at times.'

Pam, like Douglas, died in 2009, but when I spoke to her just a few weeks before, she said: 'I have so many good memories of Hickstead. We had our ups and downs, of course, but I did enjoy working there. It was the making of my life.'

Douglas was a man of such positive views, about almost everything but especially if it involved his beloved showground, that a discussion could easily develop into a fierce argument. But the ill-feeling subsided as quickly as it welled up. Once, when I wrote in one of my reports for *The Daily Telegraph* something about the poor state of the ground, an incensed Douglas threatened to bar me from the show; the next day I, of course, turned up as usual, and his first remark was 'come and have a drink'. A lot of drink was taken at Hickstead over the years, invariably of the highest quality, as Douglas's cellar was justly famous.

Douglas spent fortunes, not far short of £1million, in continually improving the ground in the International Arena, and in recent years his son Edward—who looks after all six arenas on the showground—has made producing the best possible surface his number one priority. Nick Skelton, winner of three Derbies and four King's Cups among other major competitions there, is in no doubt about the result: 'When you've had two good weeks of sunshine beforehand and Edward has watered it, it's probably the best jumping ground in the world. Okay, when you get rain it deteriorates a little bit, but I still prefer jumping on grass to anything else. I think a lot of horses have been spoilt by all-weather surfaces—they've got soft.'

Douglas and Pam's partnership, albeit a slightly lop-sided one, lasted many years, and Pam went on to build courses at many international shows, including Ron and Marg Southern's Spruce Meadows International in Calgary, Canada, which, as the Southerns have said, was inspired by Hickstead.

Jon Doney succeeded Pam—he is now a regular judge at Hickstead and beyond—and since 2000 the principal course-designers have been Kelvin Bywater and Bob Ellis, who was assistant to Jon for some years previously, not just at Hickstead

Pamela Carruthers, Hickstead's first course designer

Douglas Bunn rode daily around the Hickstead estate well into his seventies.

but at such important competitions as the 1994 World Championships in The Hague. Hickstead is clearly a great 'shop window', as Bob also is in constant demand at shows around the world. A rider before he took to course designing, he frequently competed at Hickstead and was a member of the show-jumping team that won the 1975 cross-country—the second running of another of Douglas's innovations that has since, in the guise of team chasing, become so widely popular.

Longevity is a feature of Hickstead officialdom. Bob Warren was show director almost from the outset until, after the World Championships in 1974, he decided to retire, and Douglas asked John Farmer, who is still there, to take over.

John—who had started stewarding there when one of the regulars failed to turn up—and gradually became more involved, recalls one of his earliest tasks, which illustrates Douglas's imaginative skills, and his obstinacy: 'Douglas drew up the first Working Hunter ring. Dorian Williams was the judge and I was asked to steward. It caused a tremendous amount of controversy because he had built a Cornish (stone) wall, and working hunters had never jumped a Cornish wall. There was an outcry, people were saying all sorts of awful things, but then it started. And who was the first person in the ring? Douglas Bunn. He jumped all the new fences, flew them and it silenced everyone.'

He said: 'For me Hickstead has always been about excellence, in all things. Douglas had incredible style. He wanted everything to be the very best, and he achieved that. George Morris (long-serving chef d'équipe of the United States team) rates this as the best showground arena in the world.'

Douglas was happy to put his expertise and enthusiasm at the service of show jumping in general, not just his own showground, and in 1969 he was elected as chairman of the British Show Jumping Association (BSJA). That was also the year that he invited Ladbrokes, then, as now, one of the country's biggest bookmakers, to bet at

Hickstead. There had been a bookmaker in the early days, which those of us who liked to bet found perhaps too beneficial, as he did not last long. Ladbrokes were on a much bigger scale, but there was considerable opposition to betting on show jumping from some of the senior members of the BSJA, and after a year Douglas' chairmanship was ended. As it happened, so did the betting, as the International Equestrian Federation brought in a rule that only Tote betting was allowed for international competitions. That rule has since been changed, and Hickstead now again has a resident bookmaker, Bet 365, while Douglas was re-elected chairman of the BSJA from 1993-1996, and was President from 2001-2005.

I think it fair to say he did not always get the official recognition he deserved, so I am delighted, particularly in retrospect, that in 2008, my last year as chairman of the British Equestrian Writers' Association, we gave him the Liz Dudden Trophy, for his outstanding contribution to equestrian sport. Little did we know then that that would be our last chance to do so, and it was especially appropriate as Liz took over from Pam Macgregor-Morris as press officer at Hickstead, until her all-too-premature death. Liz is remembered at Hickstead with a memorial trophy in her name being awarded to the winner of the Speed Derby. As another example of longevity among Hickstead officials, Peter Jeffery, who succeeded Liz, has presided over the press office for the past 23 years, and brought about many changes, especially in the sphere of communication—today's wi-fi broadband is a far cry from the telephone on a tree trunk we started with.

Regional television was quick to spot the picturesque qualities of the All England Jumping Course, as well as the excitement of the sport there, but the big viewing break-through came in 1971, when, as a result of the enthusiasm of one of sport's greatest all-round commentators, David Coleman—who became and remains a director of Hickstead—the BBC showed the first Nations Cup to be held there. Although this was

Television commentator Dorian Williams, the 'voice of show jumping' when the BBC first covered Hickstead

LEFT: Douglas Bunn congratulates his daughter Theresa after her success in the 14.2hh Championship at Hickstead.
RIGHT: Chloe Bunn and Citi Dancer, on their way to victory in the British Speed Derby in 1999

an 'unofficial' competition—as described in detail in the chapter on Nations Cups—there was a tremendous atmosphere there, a huge crowd, and BBC television had a producer, Alan Mouncer, whom Douglas described as 'a genius', who was able to show off the beauty of the course and the thrill of the competition magnificently.

Dorian Williams and later Raymond Brooks-Ward were the BBC show-jumping commentators then. Mike Tucker, former event rider and a member of the Beaufort Hunt quintet which won a team cross-country at Hickstead, who currently fills that rôle as part of the Sky team who have taken over the television coverage, said: 'Hickstead is such an exciting place to commentate at because it's a theatre. It's one of the few places (in Britain) where you get some of the world's top riders, and whoever is in the Derby it is always dramatic. Sky's innovative plans and modern technology should make the pictures even more spectacular.'

Most of the major problems during Hickstead's first 50 years have been financial ones, and 1980 was especially critical when W.D. & H.O. Wills, who had been almost the sole sponsors for 20 years, decided to end their connection. Douglas, ever optimistic, saw this as: 'The start of bigger and better things'. He decided that the way forward was to have different sponsors of each meeting, of which there were four at that time, and had already netted Everest Double Glazing as one of them.

Douglas was not wrong to be optimistic, even though the new regime meant continuing to dig deep into the Bunn exchequer: the following year's Hambro Life British Jumping Derby carried what was then British show jumping's biggest-ever prize-money, £34,000; by 2009, with DFS in their sixth year of sponsorship, the Derby was worth a total of £120,000.

Hickstead these days has just two International shows a year—plus the long-standing National Schools and Pony Club Jumping Championships. With Longines continuing as the title sponsor of the Royal International Horse Show and of the King George V Gold Cup, which in 2009 had its prize-money raised to an impressive £162,500—as it had to be, to conform to the requirements of the new FEI Meydan Nations Cup series—Hickstead offers richer pickings than ever.

But it could all have ground to a halt in 1997. Silk Cut, who had followed W.D. & H.O. Wills in sponsoring at Hickstead for 16 years, ended their support when it became known that the Government was about to ban sports sponsorship by tobacco companies. Existing contracts were allowed to continue until they ran out, but that between Silk Cut and Hickstead was coming to an end, and because of the upcoming ban could not be renewed. Douglas appealed in vain to the Sports Council to help fill the £400,000 hole left by Silk Cut's departure. As a result the Nations Cup was transferred to the Royal Windsor Horse Show amid very real fears that the remainder of the Royal International Horse Show, and the British Jumping Derby, would be lost completely. Douglas had been putting some £200,000 or more of his own money into Hickstead each year, and now said: 'My accountant told me I couldn't remain show jumping's John Paul Getty II forever, and I have taken his advice.'

Help was forthcoming, however, from his old friend Paul Schockemöhle, winner of three Derbies and a European Championship at Hickstead, and by then a highly

> *'It is not an exaggeration to say that without Hickstead there would have been no Spruce Meadows. In this respect we owe a great debt of gratitude to Douglas for his passion and wide sphere of influence.'*
>
> LINDA SOUTHERN-HEATHCOTT
> (President and CEO of Spruce Meadows, Calgary)

successful businessman. Said Paul: 'Hickstead is one of the biggest jumping facilities in the whole world—a unique place. Douglas Bunn was a tough sportsman, he rode himself and was very ambitious for the show. He was a horseman and that is why he succeeded. There is a fantastic atmosphere over here and the public have realised this. That's why they called him the Master of Hickstead. I came in to help when the government forbade cigarette sponsorship of sport, and Silk Cut was then almost his only sponsor, so it was difficult for him to keep the show going. I have a marketing agency in Germany so I tried to help, but finally he did it himself, and his whole family have brought the show together again. And that's good, because I think without Hickstead the whole show-jumping world would be a lot poorer than it is now.' The Royal International Horse Show, without the Nations Cup on that occasion but with the King George V and the Queen Elizabeth II Cups and a variety of sponsors, and the Derby, sponsored by Peugeot, were saved, and have thrived ever since.

Perhaps what made Douglas happiest of all was that, as Paul Schockemöhle mentioned, so many members of his family have been and remain closely involved in the running of the All England Jumping Course: in particular Edward, with his vitally important care of the arenas and general running of the shows, Lizzie and John, and the children of his third wife, Lorna, whom he married in 1979, Chloe, Daisy and Charlie. A fourth child, Douglas, died in infancy. All are directors; Lizzie is also the organising secretary, Daisy looks after the sponsorship and John runs the polo, being a keen player himself. Chloe followed her father in studying law and in riding successfully, including winning the 1999 Speed Derby on Douglas's Citi Dancer, one of the most emotional of results for him.

Now Chloe and her husband Shane Breen—winner of the 2006 Eventing Grand Prix and the British Speed Derby and Queen Elizabeth II Cup in 2008—run the British side of their expanding equestrian business (with Shane's brother Trevor and their father John in charge in Ireland), as well as bringing up their two daughters, Lorna and Darcy, at Hickstead.

Douglas's sad death just before the 2009 Derby meeting, with his funeral being held the day after, brought together many of those who had played a part, big or small, in his and Hickstead's life, during half a century. The many friendships he had established, the respect he had gained for what he had done and for what he was, was so clearly shown by the huge gathering; and the party afterwards was just the sort that he enjoyed, and gave so often. Douglas Bunn created Hickstead and saw it safely through its many vicissitudes: his family will make sure that the tradition continues.

> *'Hickstead really inspired me into show jumping. I came here as a kid, probably four or five years old, when my father was jumping, as an amateur, in the outside rings. Cantering into the main ring for the first time was awesome, and whatever else Duggie has left, the Derby is special; the big Bank, the ditches, the Derby fences set it aside from anything else. It brings show jumping home to the people.'*
>
> WILLIAM FUNNELL

OPPOSITE PAGE: Douglas Bunn's coffin being carried into Hurstpierpoint College Chapel by his fellow show jumpers (right to left) John Whitaker, Michael Whitaker and Peter Charles: on the other side were his son-in-law Shane Breen, William Funnell and Geoff Billington, watched by members of the Hickstead staff.

Remembering Hickstead, by Bill Steinkraus

(Winner of the Individual Gold Medal at the Mexico Olympic Games and long-serving captain of the United States Jumping Team)

Douglas Bunn's original concept for Hickstead developed after World War II in response to certain pressing needs of the British equestrian community. American show jumpers shared these very same pressing needs—the means of developing horses and riders who could cope with European/Olympic style show-jumping obstacles and courses, scored under the rules of the Belgium-based International Equestrian Federation (FEI). Prior to 1950, both the British and the American civilian riders conducted most domestic jumping competitions under their own, historic but very different rules, in which touches ('ticks') were scored as well as knockdowns and disobediences, over relatively small obstacles in a relatively confined space, with elapsed time only rarely a scoring factor. Suffice it to say that once civilian organizations became responsible for fielding Olympic equestrian teams following the dissolution of most cavalry-trained military teams, there was a very steep learning curve in adjusting to the new rules and competitive conditions.

Considering everything, the American and British show jumpers got to where they could cope relatively quickly, in any case significantly faster than could have been possible without the invaluable contributions of Douglas Bunn, Hickstead, and its principal course designer in the early years, Pam Carruthers, along with the rest of the Hickstead team. The U.S. team also benefited enormously from obtaining the services as coach and trainer of the Hungarian-born cavalry officer and brilliant horseman, Bertalan de Nemethy, later to be an Olympic course designer himself.

On the technical side, riding at Hickstead was from the beginning a hugely educational experience for our horses and riders, for Douglas was a very progressive thinker about jumpers, rules and jumper courses, and quickly caught up with what they were doing in Europe at such great shows as Aachen. Drawing from the best that he had seen abroad, Douglas quickly established Hickstead as one of the great show-jumping venues in the world, playing a role that was much admired and became enormously influential. (Over time, it also inspired many similar projects elsewhere in the world, perhaps most notably at Spruce Meadows in Canada, where Pam Carruthers was also involved. This wide spread of the higher standards exemplified by Hickstead was surely one of its most important contributions to the whole equestrian community.) In the first iteration at Hickstead, Douglas introduced all of the special continental types of obstacles that were used in

The United States team at Hickstead: (left to right) Carole Hoffman, Frank Chapot, Mary Chapot, Bill Steinkraus, Kathy Kusner and Billy Robertson

Europe, singly and in combination—a variety of ditches and water jumps, all sorts of banks from little singles to the huge Hickstead Bank patterned after Hamburg, Liverpools, Budapesters (think 'Devil's Dyke')—you name it. And then Douglas created his own showcase for them all, the now legendary Hickstead Derby.

Unforgettable though the showground and its contents were, the human side of the Hickstead experience was even more memorable, for Douglas made visiting riders feel almost like members of his own family. Indeed, senior judges, coaches and team captains with their wives were often invited to stay with the Bunns during the show, and in our case, riders, too, were often accommodated if there was an interval between shows in England and the continent. Other visitors were put up nearby, the younger riders sometimes staying in caravans, but many were still invited to join the group for meals in the main house, read the newspapers—Douglas got them all—and discuss the developments of the day, equine and other. At night after dinner, port was often served and there was always lots of good talk, for Douglas was a very good talker and a very determined advocate for his own positions. (He was, after all, trained as a barrister.) The serious talk started at dinner and eventually moved to the living room where we rejoined the wives. However, long after the distaff members had retired upstairs the talk was still going strong, especially if there were controversial matters to discuss and there was no show the next day.

Watching Hickstead evolve during the couple of decades when I was privileged to ride there regularly and on the odd visits thereafter were among the great highlights of my riding career during a very precious era in our sport. Much has changed since Hickstead's early days, and equestrian sport has experienced many bumps in the road along the way. Douglas found a way to involve Hickstead with the dressage community, and even the eventers, and the whole operation these days is infinitely larger and more complex. It is very reassuring to see the active participation of the next generation of Bunns in Hickstead's present-day activities, however, and to observe that the show's role in England and in the international equestrian scene in general is more prominent than ever.

Thirty-odd years ago, Douglas was kind enough to provide a brief chapter for a book I edited covering the early years of the United States Equestrian Team in which he very generously noted what he felt the USET had contributed to show jumping up to that point. I can only say that its success in those years and subsequently could never have been obtained so quickly without the solid foundation in the European style of show jumping we were able to obtain during those early Hickstead years, thanks to Douglas's far-sightedness and unstinting generosity. I am certain that those of us who experienced his friendship personally will always treasure it.

Bill Steinkraus, elegant as ever in the saddle, on Snowbound in the 1964 British Jumping Derby

The Championships

'...Hickstead's unique International Arena has found the weaknesses in other good horses before and since, as well as bringing out the best in those who can adapt.'

1974 – STEENKEN'S WORLD CHAMPIONSHIP

It did not take long for the International Equestrian Federation (FEI) to recognise the immense promise that Hickstead held for the long-term future of show jumping, especially of course in Britain but also as a pattern for the international sport. And just one year after the All England Jumping Course opened the FEI decided that the 1961 European Junior Jumping Championships should be held there.

They were the first of many, at all age levels and including dressage as well as jumping, to have been since staged at the Sussex showground, with the most important being the 1974 World Men's Championship. And there could not have been a more appropriate venue for it.

Britain had earned the right to stage the World Men's Championship in 1974—the last year in which separate championships were held for men and women, as from the following season they were, as now, mixed—by the victory four years earlier in La Baule of David Broome and Beethoven, owned by the 'Master of Hickstead', Douglas Bunn.

Beethoven deserves to have his own story told, and will have it, but enough here to acknowledge the debt that Hickstead owes him in getting these ground-breaking championships. Max E. Ammann, in his recent book *The FEI Championships* credits those in La Baule and Hickstead with being the most important in creating media interest in a sport that, hitherto, had commanded little. Certainly for the next couple of decades media interest in equestrian sport, and especially show jumping, was at its peak.

But the 1974 renewal might well not have happened, or at least could have been robbed of some of the main protagonists, when the International Olympic Committee, in their investigations before bringing in a new standard of eligibility for the Olympic Games, suggested that amateurs should not be allowed to compete against professionals.

This would have meant that Broome, together with the other two British riders, Harvey Smith and Paddy McMahon, could be barred, or else that many of their possible rivals, still clinging to an illusion of amateurism (merely because their own national federations had, unlike the British, allowed them to maintain that status) would pull out rather than risk being disqualified from future Olympics.

When Colonel Sir Mike Ansell, who ran British show jumping with steely but highly effective determination, learned of this threat, which only arose in the immediate lead-up to the championships, he sought urgent clarification of the situation, and was assured by Lord Killanin, whose Presidency of the IOC was sadly short-lived, but who was undoubtedly one of the most honourable holders of that position, that whatever ruling his committee might bring in, it would not be retrospective.

So the championships could go ahead, untrammelled by pettifogging regulation, and produced a contest which to this day remains memorable. Truly a contest of giants.

The World Championships began in 1953 and right from the start the formula was controversial: it still is, but remains virtually unchanged, and consists of three qualifying rounds, with the top four riders at the end of those rounds going in to a final in which each of them rides all four horses, and the rider with the least faults emerging victorious. In every other championship it is the combination of rider and horse that wins, but the World title belongs more to the rider, and having the best horse may, in the final, be a disadvantage.

In the second championship, in Madrid, the winner of the first, Spain's Paco Goyoaga, was allowed in to the change-of-horse finale together with the four qualifiers. That idea was dropped, but even in 1974 the holder, David Broome, was allowed automatically to defend his title, in addition to the two riders each country was permitted to enter, but then had to earn his place in the finale.

Harvey Smith had been with him in La Baule, and finished third there, when they were the first two riders from the same country ever to qualify for a final. Smith, after a quiet early season in 1974, had timed his horse Salvador's preparation for the championships to a

PAGE 26: The finalists in the 1974 World Men's Championship: (left to right) Hartwig Steenken on Simona, Eddie Macken on Pele, Hugo Simon on Lavendel, and Frank Chapot on Main Spring

COURSE PLANS FOR THE 1974 WORLD MEN'S CHAMPIONSHIP

FIRST ROUND:
Round One: Table C (against the clock).
Fences up to 4ft 11in (1.50m)

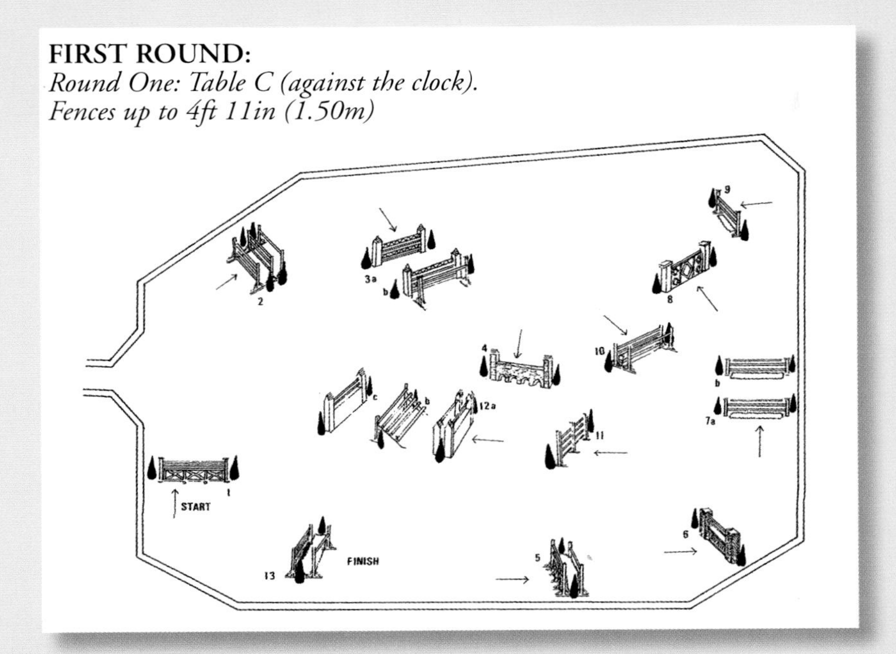

SECOND ROUND:
Initial round and one jump-off, not against the clock.
Fences up to 5ft 9in (1.75m)

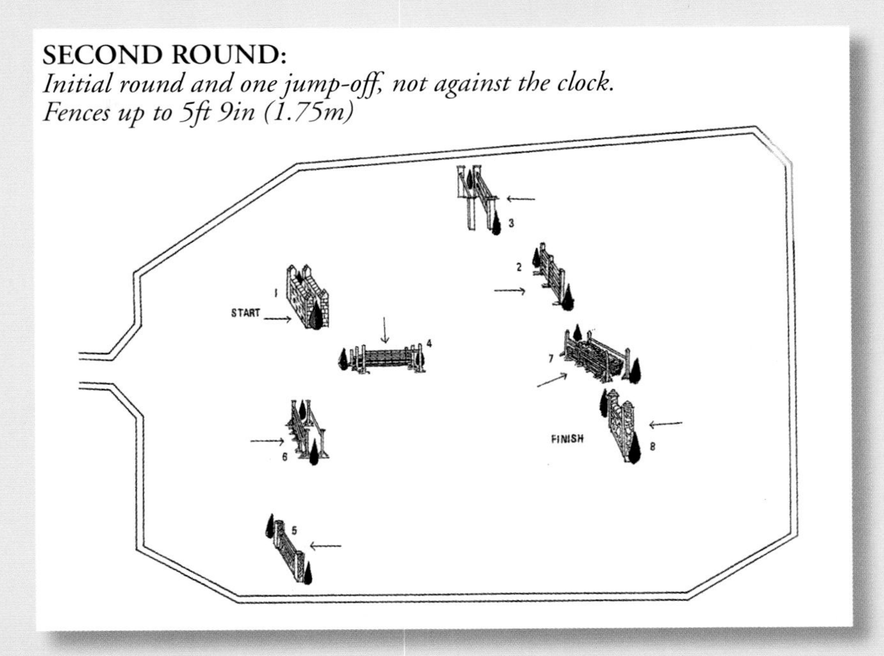

THIRD ROUND:
Nations Cup (two rounds not against the clock).
Fences up to 5ft 3in (1.60m)

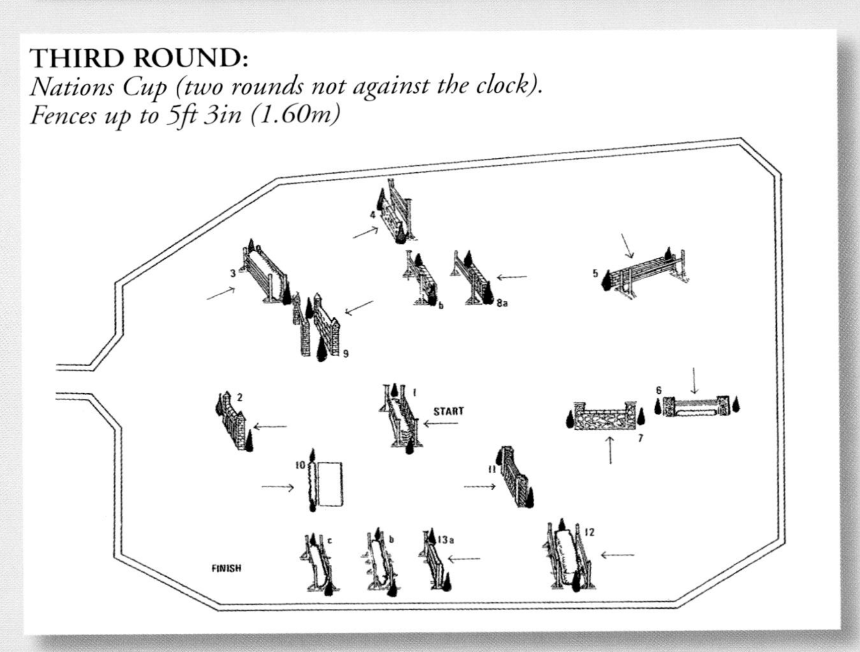

FINAL ROUND:
Change of horses.
Fences up to 4ft 11in (1.50m).

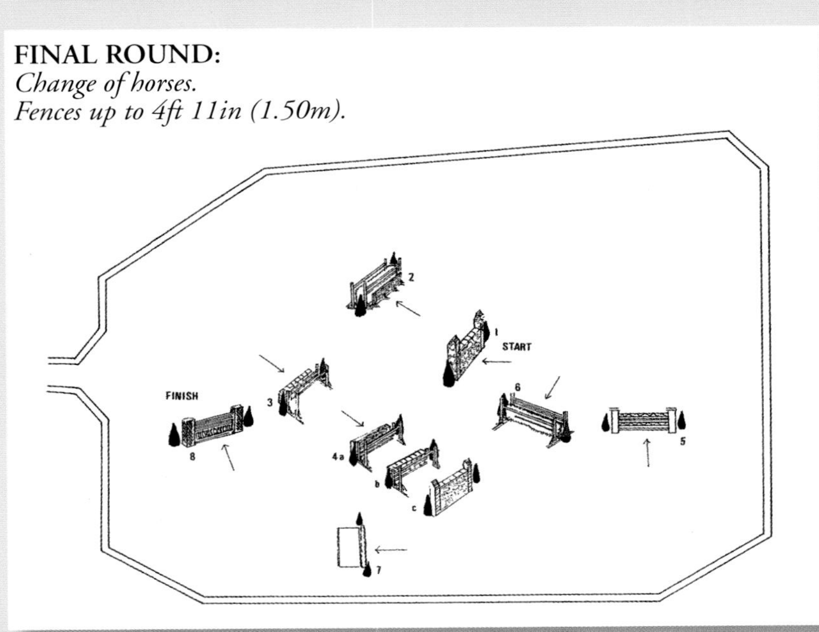

Hartwig Steenken on Simona at the World Men's Championships, 1974

nicety and so was chosen for Britain together with Paddy McMahon who, with Pennwood Forge Mill, had won the European Championship at Hickstead in 1973.

In 1970 Broome had thought long and hard over which horse to ride in the Championships before opting for the potential brilliance of the unproven-at-that-level Beethoven, and again he was in something of a dilemma. Sportsman, his No 1, had been suffering from minor back trouble and there was no way of knowing whether the treatment, including swimming, he had been given would enable him to hold up through the three qualifiers and, if he got there, the final.

Broome's alternative was the young American-bred Philco, owned as was Sportsman by Phil (now Lord) Harris. In the end the Welshman decided on Sportsman, and the gamble so nearly came off, for they failed by just one place to reach the final four.

The starting field was the biggest up to that time, with 29 riders from 16 countries, and right from the start it was clear that Hickstead's resident course designer, Pam Carruthers, would test them to the limit.

Indeed, most of the horses would be tested beyond what they were capable of, for the tracks were so demanding that only the very best horses could jump them clear, with limited possibilities for riders, no matter how skilful, to compensate for their horses' shortcomings. So it was not surprising that those horses who could cope with the demands of the courses dominated from start to finish.

They were not necessarily all horses that were most loudly touted beforehand, but the eventual winner, Hartwig Steenken, with his gallant and talented mare Simona, was certainly among the ante post favourites.

Steenken and Simona, who was 16 years old in 1974, had won the European Championship in 1971 and were members of Germany's gold medal team at the Munich Olympics, when they finished equal fourth individually—as did Hugo Simon and

Lavendel, who also reached the 1974 final—a mere 0.75 of a fault behind the three who jumped off for the medals.

It was a very mixed field, in terms of both ability and experience, and something of a watershed, with some riders, like 24-year-old New Zealander John Cottle for example at the beginning of their international careers—though he quickly made his mark around the British circuit—and others, like the supreme d'Inzeo brothers, Raimondo and Piero, coming towards the end of theirs.

Raimondo d'Inzeo had already won the World Championship twice, in 1956 and 1960, having been second in 1955, and was still in winning Nations Cup teams for Italy in 1977, but for some reason he never shone at Hickstead, and once again showed it was not his favourite stamping ground.

From the United States came one man, Frank Chapot, who was already a regular and highly successful rider in Europe, including at Hickstead—and has gone on to be the U.S. team manager—and another, Rodney Jenkins, competing in Europe for the first time. He was riding the 'talking horse' of the championships, Idle Dice, who at that time had won more prize-money than any other show jumper in the world.

Jenkins was the first professional to ride for the U.S. team, and with his federation's publicity machine proclaiming him 'the best in the world', he had plenty to live up to. Sadly he and Idle Dice did not live up to it, but Hickstead's unique International Arena has found the weaknesses in other good horses before and since, as well as bringing out the best in those who can adapt.

From Ireland came a young rider, 24-year-old Eddie Macken, who was later to prove just how effective he was around Hickstead, with four successive victories, from 1976 to 79, on Boomerang in the British Jumping Derby.

He came in to the World Championship with a problem somewhat similar to Broome's—whether or not to rely on a horse with brilliant potential but as-yet little experience at such a high level, the seven-year-old Pele, or one of either Oatfield Hills or Easter Parade, his mounts in the previous year's European Championships, when he finished ninth.

All three were owned by Macken's mentor and trainer, Iris Kellett, who won the Queen Elizabeth II Cup in 1949 and 1951, ran a training centre in Dublin, and made a comeback to top competition to win the Women's European Championship in 1969.

Between them they opted for the more courageous course and chose Pele, and from the start this proved the correct decision, and underlined what d'Oriola had shown with Pomone in 1966 and Broome with Beethoven in 1970, that brilliance can overcome lack of experience, while moderate horses do not win championships.

Pele had been successful in ridden hunter championships in Belfast and Dublin before

Rodney Jenkins on Idle Dice at the World Men's Championship, 1974

his attention was turned to jumping, and the training he had had was put to good use in the first of the three qualifying rounds of the World Championships, which, as always, was against the clock from the start and which, invariably, had a crucial effect upon the final placings. Although a good start could be frittered away in the subsequent rounds, a bad one leaves ground almost impossible to make up.

Macken and Pele were not just good, they were marvellous. The 13-fence course that Pam Carruthers had designed for the opening leg used Hickstead's huge arena to the full, but it was not one that riders could just gallop round and hope for the best. It demanded total concentration from both horse and rider, but Macken and Pele made it look almost easy.

Round they went, with rapier-like precision and never a semblance of a jumping error, to clock a time, 95.6sec, that beat the next best, Simon with Lavendel, by the massive margin of 3.5sec. Simon had at one time ridden for Germany, where he was born, but when he was overlooked for their teams he changed to his parents' Austrian nationality. There must have been many times when the German selectors wished he had stayed with them.

Only four went clear, with Steenken and Simona taking third place in 101.3sec, but the fourth faultless round, by Edward Cuepper's Le Champion, was so slow as to leave them only seventh, behind three who had to add seven seconds for a fence down. Fastest of these, for fourth place, were Paddy McMahon and Pennwood Forge Mill.

The pattern set on that opening day was to stay more-or-less in place throughout the championships, but still it was an amazing feat that the first four in the speed round, and they alone, all finished equal first in the second leg, when sheer jumping power was at a premium.

Only 22 horses were left in for the third and final qualifier, run in Nations Cup-style with two rounds over a long, 13-fence course that ended with a stamina-draining treble. No surprise that only one horse could jump it clear twice, the phenomenal Simona. First time she never put a foot wrong, and although in the second round she was on a wrong stride after jumping the water, such was her scope that she easily cleared the balustrade that came soon afterwards.

It says much for the consistency of both the courses and the horses that once again, with one sad exception, the same ones emerged triumphant. Pele and Lavendel were also clear in the first round. But for McMahon and Pennwood Forge Mill, the fourth of the big four from the two previous rounds, this proved a day to forget. At no stage in the first round did the horse look happy, and he may have already been suffering pain from the neck injury that was to sideline him a little later. Rattling and bouncing his way along, he was at least still clear coming to the last, but the treble got to the bottom of this gallant campaigner.

He struggled over the first two elements, but stopped at the third; brought round again, he hit the first part, and just clambered over the next two. Seven faults, plus four and a quarter for time, was bad enough, but the second round was even worse, with three fences down, which dropped him from the top four to 15th.

In that second round, while Simona romped clear to win, both Pele and Lavendel showed the slightest of chinks in their armour, to finish equal second with one mistake apiece.

But McMahon's misfortune meant that the fourth place in the final was up for grabs. It went to Frank Chapot on Main Spring, who had only one down each time, and he joined Steenken, Macken and Simon. All started from scratch and would test their horsemanship in the World Championship's unique, horse-swapping formula, with each rider having three minutes to get to know each of their opponents' horses before going in to jump.

Often in these finals the rider with the best, most consistent, horse, is at a disadvantage, but the standard of the four horses in the 1974 final was so high that no rider had a particular advantage or disadvantage.

Pam Carruthers' course for the final, of just eight fences, was naturally much less

ABOVE: Frank Chapot on Main Spring
TOP RIGHT: Hugo Simon on Lavendel
BOTTOM RIGHT: Eddie Macken on Pele at the World Men's Championships, 1974

demanding than the three qualifying rounds had been, but still asked questions enough. Each of the four rode their own horses first, with Simon and Lavendel leading the way with an easy clear. Indeed all four went round without fault, but Chapot was at his strongest to ensure that the wily Main Spring did not run out, as he sometimes could, and although Macken and Pele had a couple of interesting moments when rapping the first element of the treble and then being slightly out of their stride at the next, they were never in serious danger of collecting any faults.

Steenken was last to go, and rode with an eye to the immediate future, by letting the headstrong Simona stride on as fast as was safe, rather than trying to calm her down. She tanked round like a steeplechaser, had to be steadied for the last, but flew every fence with ease.

Lavendel could pull a bit, too, and Chapot, his rider in the second round, spent the three-minute practice session sawing at the horse's mouth, determined not to let him get into top gear. It almost worked, as they were clear until hitting the sixth, an oxer that caused most of the problems. Macken lowered the same fence on Main Spring, and was kicking himself afterwards as this veteran thoroughbred was the one of the three horses that he said he felt most at home on.

It is difficult to imagine two more different rides than the strong, experienced Simona and the young, athletic Pele, but Steenken got on so well with the Irish horse that he did not need his full three minutes practice before setting off on a clear round. Simon had plenty on his hands with Simona, and tried to make it a battle of strength, from which there could be only one winner. But though the mare took charge, she never liked hitting

FROM LEFT TO RIGHT: Hartwig Steenken on (i) Simona, (ii) Main Spring, (iii) Pele, (iv) Lavendel

fences, and despite having a scary trip through the treble, faulted only at the difficult sixth.

So at halfway Steenken had a four-fault lead over the other three, but Macken (on Lavendel) and Chapot (on Simona) levelled the score when going clear in the next round, while Steenken and Main Spring kicked out the bogey fence, the sixth. Simon dropped back to last, though only by four faults, when Pele made a rare error at the water.

Steenken and Lavendel were first to go in the final round: it was not a fluent round as they could easily have had two down, and Lavendel looked as though he wanted to stop at the last, but did not, and cleared it. Simon, now with no chance of winning, had a relaxed clear on Main Spring, but Pele, having found that landing in the water did him no harm with Simon in the saddle, did it again for Chapot.

So the American's chance was also gone, when Macken came in last on Simona. If the mare could have read her usual rider's mind, no doubt she would have hit something, and indeed she did not make it easy for the Irishman, with her head down almost between her knees and putting in such prodigious leaps that Macken could have been hurled out of the saddle had he not sat like a limpet. At the last it looked as though Simona was going to answer Steenken's prayers when she took off a full stride from the fence, but somehow she found a mid-air turbo boost to carry her over.

This left Chapot and Simon equal third, and Steenken and Macken to jump-off for the title, the first time this had happened since 1955. The barrage was over the full course, with Macken having to go first. Knowing he had to go all out, he cut an audacious short track to the third, and over, and again to the sixth, but hit it. Then, having obviously got a taste for it, Pele, until this day a fabulous water jumper, splashed his way in: they were fast, but with

an eight-fault target Steenken and Simona could now have a fence down and still win.

And they did, when the mare also landed on the tape at the water, but Steenken, the day before his 33rd birthday, was crowned World Champion in front of a huge crowd, and received his trophy from Princess Anne.

There was a sad sequel to this, one of the most dramatic of championships, however, when three years later Steenken was so badly injured in a car crash that, after clinging to life for months, he died in January 1978.

1965 – MARION ON TOP OF THE WORLD

Only three World Championships confined to women riders were held, and Hickstead staged the first of them, in 1965. The others followed in 1970, in Copenhagen, and 1974 in La Baule.

Only eight riders lined up, but what the field lacked in quantity it more than made up for in quality. Top riders came from Europe, Ireland and North and South America, including US rider Kathy Kusner who was in tremendous form but who, after three hectic days of close competition for the title, had to give pride of place to the youngest rider and smallest horse, 18-year-old Marion Coakes on Stroller, who stood just under 14.2 hands high.

Marion and Stroller formed a combination suited to perfection by Hickstead's formidable obstacles, but even before Stroller came into her life Marion had already shown her liking for the showground in its inaugural year, 1960, on her good 13.2 pony Music. At the end of that year her father Ralph bought Stroller to take her up through the ranks—as they thought then—of pony and junior competition. Neither of them could have imagined just how high up the show-jumping ladder they would ascend—eventually to an Olympic silver medal in Mexico, with a plethora of other important prizes before that, and afterwards.

Marion (later Mrs Mould, wife of the distinguished National Hunt jockey David) and Stroller soon made their mark in junior competitions, and were among the team that won the 1962 European Junior Championship in Berlin when they had to go last and jumped a superb clear to clinch the title. But it was when they encountered the much bigger fences of senior competition that Stroller's latent ability became clear to all.

In July 1965 Marion and Stroller had thrilled the packed spectators at the Royal International Horse Show, then held at the White City, when winning the Queen Elizabeth II Cup by just 0.1sec—the smallest margin for the smallest ever winning equine—from Alison Westwood (later Mrs Dawes) on The Maverick, another duo destined for Hickstead Derby glory. And these two combinations were chosen to represent Britain in the World Championship.

Unlike the men's world championships, the women's were run under the more conventional lines of the European formula, with three rounds and the leader at the end of them being the winner.

Marion and Stroller's glory days were, for the most part, still ahead of them, and going in to the championship Kathy Kusner and Untouchable were firm favourites. Kathy, a 25-year-old Virginian, had ridden Untouchable in the United States Olympic teams in Tokyo and Mexico, where they missed a medal by just one place. But favourites do not always win, and it was the British riders who dominated the opening, speed round of the championships; and although there were only the two of them they filled the top three places. Each rider was allowed, if she wished, to ride two horses, and Marion took Little Fellow as well as Stroller.

Pam Carruthers, as always, was determined to test this small but talented field to the utmost; not necessarily with huge fences, though the 15 included some that were formidable enough, but in the way she arranged them, with many twists and turns. And with seven seconds being added for every fence down, there was no room for error.

Little Fellow was hardly appropriately-named as he stood 16.1hh, nearly two hands

OPPOSITE PAGE: Raimondo d'Inzeo on Bellevue at the World Men's Championships, 1974

Marion Mould with Stroller at his retirement ceremony. Stroller had 15 years of happy retirement before he died of a heart attack, aged 36, in 1986.

higher than his illustrious stablemate, and although he never reached the same heights as Stroller he was a more than useful second string. Going second in the competition he set a decent enough standard, clear in 77.5sec, but was comprehensively eclipsed by Alison Westwood and The Maverick, who galloped round in 72.9sec.

Marion and Stroller needed to take risks to beat their time, and did just that, by 1.2sec, having their share of luck along the way as they rattled, but did not dislodge, a number of fences. Between them the two British riders had the only clear rounds.

Kathy Kusner, on the other hand, was out of luck, for she and the ex-racehorse Untouchable were just about fastest of all turning in to the last fence, but there, for a fleeting moment, the horse hesitated, took off on a bad stride and for once could not jump his way out of trouble. Even with the extra seven seconds, they were fourth, and so third in the championship as only the best horse of each rider counted.

Right from the outset this was a three-woman contest for places on the podium, and the top spot was put beyond much doubt during the second round, when Marion finished equal first on Stroller and Little Fellow.

This was a Nations Cup-type competition, with two rounds over 13 fences, of which five stood at a maximum 4ft 11in, and a 15 ½ft water jump. Marion had one fence down on both Stroller and Little Fellow, as did Alison on The Maverick and Kathy with Untouchable.

When they all went round again Marion had both her horses spot on at every fence, to finish on two-round totals of four with each of them. Untouchable repeated his first round four faults but Alison dropped behind her when The Maverick, with unaccustomed inaccuracy, had two down and a stop.

Going in to the third and final leg of the championships, with Marion leading on two points and Alison and Kathy sharing second on five, it looked as though only a major mishap could prevent her from taking the first ever Women's World Championship.

So it proved, though not without a few moments of worry for the Coakes camp. Marion could only ride one horse in this final leg, and naturally enough chose Stroller to face a marathon first course, of 18 fences, of which six were taken out for the second round.

The field was now down to just five riders, and Kathy Kusner with her brilliant veteran thoroughbred Untouchable had the only clear in the exhausting first round. Stroller had two fences down and The Maverick three, leaving Alison with little chance of grabbing the title.

She was never one to give up, however, and over the last course of the championships she and The Maverick went faultlessly. Untouchable dropped a foot in the water, but Stroller reverted to his normal immaculate jumping and gave Britain a second clear, and Marion Coakes was crowned the first Woman World Champion.

EUROPEAN CHAMPIONSHIPS

1961 – Sheila Barnes, top junior

Championship jumping at Hickstead had begun just a year after the showground was opened, when the International Equestrian Federation (FEI) awarded them the 1961 European Championship for Juniors.

Although it took the FEI until 1975 to open the senior championships to both men and women, and to introduce team competitions, the junior championships, which started two years earlier than the seniors, in 1952, were mixed, for boys and girls, from the start. At the beginning they only had a team title to aim at, but in London in 1959, when the British team completed a four-timer, an individual category was added, with the Duke of Norfolk's daughter Lady Sarah FitzAlan-Howard on Oorskiet, members of the winning team, sharing first place with Italy's Gualtiero Castellini on Ventuno.

Jane Kidd, Douglas Coakes—Marion's older brother—and Mike Cresswell, all of whom went on to successful senior careers, were the others in the 1959 team, and were also in that which won in 1960, together with Liz Broome, later Mrs Edgar and also, of course, a hugely successful senior rider.

But, with an upper age limit of 18, it was all change for 1961. Nine countries entered teams, though a ferocious gale that delayed Channel crossings, meant that two of them, from Hungary and Italy, did not arrive until 5a.m. on the morning the meeting started.

Britain, with an all-girl side, were rated favourites to win a sixth successive team championship, but in the end they finished only third to Germany's quartet of boys in a 'blanket finish' to a competition run during torrential rain that made the ground decidedly difficult.

All four of the Germans were riding well-schooled Hannoverian horses who coped better than their rivals with the conditions, headed by their national junior champion, Heinz von Opel, whose eight-year-old Cari jumped a double clear. Germany finished on 16 faults, 3.75 ahead of Holland with the British a quarter of a fault further behind.

But if they disappointed in the team championship, the British girls more than made up for it in the Individual Championship, in which they were the only ones to get through to the jump-off for the medals.

Janet Smith led the way on Silver Toes, but slipped on turning to the gate, and hit it. Sheila Barnes, whose family did so much for British show jumping for so long, let Sola stride out for an easy clear, and although Jabeena Maslin, who was something of a

> *'Hickstead is a magic place. The first day when I arrived it was raining (as often happens in England), but straight away I had a good feeling. This show is the perfect blend between the tradition of horses, nature and sport.'*
>
> KEVIN STAUT, EUROPEAN CHAMPION 2009

Hickstead specialist and had won on the opening day, was more than 10sec faster on Arkvar, they had a fence down in doing so. This left Althea Roger-Smith—who went on to have a fine career at senior level, married NH trainer Josh Gifford, and is mother of leading three-day event rider Tina Cook—to take second place on Fanshaw, faultless but three seconds slower than Sheila Barnes.

Britain, with a team that included Marion Coakes on Stroller and John Kidd with Copper Castle, regained the title in Berlin a year later, when Kidd also won the individual championship.

1963 – PAT SMYTHE'S HAT-TRICK

The first European Women's Championship, in Spa, Belgium, in 1957, was run using the same formula as the men's World Championship, i.e. three qualifying rounds after which the top four riders all rode each others' horses. It went to a jump-off, on the riders' second horses, before Pat Smythe beat Italy's Giulia Serventi, the first of Pat's four victories in the championships, climaxing at Hickstead in 1963.

> *'Hickstead holds a very dear place in my heart because it was my first ever international competition when I was a teenager. Hickstead is family-run and maintains a distinctly traditional British atmosphere, which I love. The Nations Cup is famous for its triple bars and scary open water, which does tend to sort the men from the mice! I've had the privilege of jumping on the Irish team there eight times in the past ten years.'*
>
> CIAN O'CONNOR

Pat was second, to Ann Townsend, in 1959, missed 1960, but regained the title in Deauville in 1961, retained it in Madrid in 1962 and so was on for a hat-trick when the championship came to Britain for the first time, in 1963.

Hickstead staged no fewer than six meetings that year, and at one of the early ones the Junior Jumping Championship went, almost unnoticed, to 15-year-old Marion Coakes on Stroller.

For the European Championship meeting in July, which also included the British Jumping Derby, television cameras were in action for the first time at the Sussex showground. So a championship success for Pat Smythe, Britain's most popular show jumping rider, could not have been more opportune, both for her and for putting Hickstead firmly on the map only three years after it was opened.

Pat was joined in the British challenge for the championship by Anneli Drummond-Hay and Merely-a-Monarch, who had proved themselves supreme in the world of three-day eventing by winning the inaugural running of Burghley in 1961, and the following Spring being victorious at Badminton.

Anneli swapped from eventing to show jumping with him because she wanted to ride in the Olympic Games, and at that time women were not allowed to ride in the Olympic event—though they were permitted by the time of the next Games in Tokyo, 1964, when Lana Dupont of the United States became the first woman to do so.

It is a measure of Merely-a-Monarch's ability that the noted racehorse trainer Fulke Walwyn once said that he thought he could have trained the horse—who was by a thoroughbred, Happy Monarch, but descended from a Fell pony—to win the Grand National. Within weeks of changing disciplines Monarch won at the Royal International Horse Show in the White City, and was to have a long and distinguished, though somewhat chequered, career as a show jumper and indeed helped Anneli win the 1968

OPPOSITE PAGE: The two tradestands next to the collecting ring in the early 1960s are a far cry from the extensive and diverse retail village that covers much of the showground these days. And the current all-weather warm-up arena is also a big improvement.

Bernard Weatherill Ltd
W. H. GIDDEN

A quintet of top British riders on their way to compete in Aachen, Germany: (left to right) Ted Edgar, Ted Williams, Pat Smythe, Wilf White and Douglas Bunn

European Women's Championship in Rome.

At Hickstead, 1963, they set an early standard in the opening leg of the championships, a speed competition with six seconds added for each fence down. The horse showed his scope when jumping out of trouble at the third, a glaring white parallel, but then clipped the first part of the second double, which dropped them eventually to fifth.

Ten riders from six countries took part, several of them with two horses, and the first clear came from Holland's Irene Jansen, who had been second to Pat in Deauville two years earlier, on Icare. It was a notable effort on this, their first visit to Hickstead, but Pat and Flanagan put them firmly in their place, cutting seven seconds off their time; and then Brazil's Arline Givaudan, on her second horse Caribe also edged ahead, to take second place.

The same riders tended to dominate the women's championships, and Germany's Helga Kohler, second in 1962, now took fourth place on Piroschka.

Pam Carruthers set a deceptive course for the second, Nations Cup, competition; 13 fences, including two combinations and a 14ft water jump, that did not look too demanding but proved to be so.

Only the two British riders were able to jump it clear twice, and did so impressively, with Pat increasing her lead over Arline Givaudan—a pupil of Nelson Pessoa who was cleaning up in the non-championship competitions, including winning the Derby on Gran Geste, owned by Mme Givaudan. Merely-a-Monarch was perhaps the most impressive of all, especially first time round when he sailed over every obstacle he came to, thus helping Anneli pull up in to third place overall.

After a fairly disastrous second round on Caribe, Arline finished equal third on her second ride, Huipil, who, like Diana Conolly-Carew for Ireland on Pepsi, had four faults in the first round and then went clear in the second. But Irene Jansen and Icare, a French-bred former trotter, who had promised so much in the opener, was soon in trouble in the

Nations Cup, and at the fourth fence slipped and fell over backwards. His 23-year-old rider remounted to finish the course, but their championship hopes were gone beyond recall and Irene dropped from third to sixth overall.

The finale was a two-rounder, over 18 and then 12 fences respectively, and Pat Smythe, who had elected to miss the Derby, which came on the rest day between the last two legs of the championship, and which she had won the previous year on Flanagan, rather than jeopardise her championship prospects, went in to it with a clear lead.

As it turned out, she needed some leeway. They only cleared the water jump narrowly in the first round but came to the final fence—a treble—still faultless, only to lower the first and third elements of it. In the second, shorter circuit, they just failed to get over the water, finishing this third championship leg on 12 faults.

Anneli and Monarch, by contrast, had got better with each succeeding leg of the contest and now had just one mistake over the 30 obstacles, and won this leg; but it was not quite good enough for second place, as Arline Givaudan's Huipil, after having two down in the first round, was clear in the second, to take second place in the leg and keep the same position overall.

This was to bring Pat Smythe's championship run to an end, but what an amazing career she had: from learning to ride in Richmond Park—and winning a pony class at the historic Richmond Royal Show in 1939—then, by sheer hard work and talent, making her own way to the top in a sport that was, until she came along, dominated by men.

Her victory at Hickstead was the end of an era, though British women were to win the title three more times, Anneli in 1968, and Ann Moore in 1971 and 1973, before the championship became a combined one in 1975. But before that happened Hickstead was to stage two more men-only European Championships, in 1969 and 1973.

There was no shortage of spectators willing to pay seven shillings and sixpence for a better view of the action!

1969 – THIRD EUROPEAN GOLD FOR BROOME AND MISTER SOFTEE

In 1969 David Broome and Mister Softee each notched a third European Championship, but not as a partnership: that had only begun in 1965, almost by chance, and for both the story had started much earlier.

Broome, son of a Welsh farmer, Fred, whose ability to spot horses with potential almost matched David's gift for riding them, was in the saddle from the age of two, wearing a special harness to prevent him falling off his Shetland pony. He made his debut in the hunting field at seven, and throughout his formative years was surrounded by all manner of ponies and horses at the family's home at Mount Ballan Manor in Gwent.

So it was hardly surprising that his talent, and that of sister Liz, now Mrs Edgar, was shown early in their show-jumping careers on a wide variety of horses, and it was on the ex-Army mount Wildfire, a horse which lived up to his name, and was bought for just £60, that David made the breakthrough in to international competition.

That was in late 1957, and after a decidedly unpromising beginning they made such progress that they were short-listed for the Rome Olympics in 1960. But in the end Wildfire stayed at home, and David rode another apparently 'awkward customer', Sunsalve, in Rome.

Sunsalve had won the 1957 Queen Elizabeth II Cup when ridden by his owner's daughter, Elizabeth Anderson, but he was too strong for her, and so was lent to the British team early in 1960 with the Olympics in mind. At first the brilliant but quirky Sunsalve was ridden by Pat Smythe, but they did not get on too well together, so the chestnut was returned to Oliver Anderson.

But Fred Broome, who had seen enough of the horse to recognise his latent ability, asked Anderson whether David could try him and had his wish granted. After a few early problems they quickly formed a formidable partnership, and within weeks went to the Royal International Horse Show—then at London's White City stadium, these days, of course, at Hickstead—and won the King George V Gold Cup, something David was to do a record-breaking five more times.

Another two victories at the Royal Dublin Horse Show ensured that Broome and Sunsalve were chosen for the British team for Rome—together with Pat Smythe and David Barker—and there they won the individual bronze medal, behind the d'Inzeo brothers, Raimondo and Piero, before travelling north to Venice where, just a week later, they again finished third, in the World Championship, also behind Raimondo d'Inzeo, this time with the very tricky mare Gowran Girl.

David and Sunsalve broke the d'Inzeos' grip on major titles when they relegated Piero with Pioneer to second place in the 1961 European Championship, held in front of the usual huge and knowledgeable crowd that throngs the Aachen, Germany, show every year.

The spectators had their money's-worth, with five riders eventually jumping off for the medals, with Sunsalve showing all his courage and brilliance when overcoming a major error at the treble to win, making David the first Briton to win the European Championship. But his efforts in Aachen took a lot out of Sunsalve, who returned to his Norfolk home to be ridden by Elizabeth Anderson, but died during the summer of 1962.

Broome, without Sunsalve but still with a worthy contender in the Hon. Janet Kidd's Grand Manan, was somewhat controversially denied the chance to defend his European title at the White City, London, when the selectors chose his Rome team-mate David Barker and Peter Robeson, two years later bronze medal winner in Tokyo, to ride for Britain instead.

Barker and Mister Softee, owned by John Massarella, one of the Yorkshire family who have played such an important part in British show jumping—most notably, of course, Ronnie, the team's highly successful chef d'équipe for so many years—ran out the clear winners, with Piero d'Inzeo second again, jointly with Germany's Hans Günter Winkler,

OPPOSITE PAGE: The Arena at Hickstead as it was in the early days—circa 1963

START

team and individual gold medal winner in the 1956 Olympics.

Fast-forward three years, during which time Broome had ridden Jacapo in the fourth-placed British Olympic team in Tokyo, 1964. Mister Softee, meanwhile, had been out of action for most of that season with a leg problem, and when David Barker was offered the ride on Bob Hansen's ex-Canadian star O'Malley early in 1965 he decided that he could not do justice to both horses, so relinquished the ride on Mister Softee.

John Lanni was John Massarella's first choice to take over, but it was not a success, and two falls at the Royal International—after the second of which Lanni was stretchered out of the arena and taken to hospital—the partnership came to an end. Fred Broome suggested to Lanni that if he wanted the horse to be given a 'confidence booster', David would pop him over a few fences, and that he did in the White City collecting ring.

A week later Massarella telephoned and asked David to take over on the horse, but it was not until the following season, 1966, that they really clicked, and won four of the country's most important competitions, the King George V Gold Cup, the British Jumping Derby, the Olympic Trial at the British Timken show, and the Horse of the Year Show championship.

An outbreak of swamp fever in France that year meant that British and Irish horses were unable to compete on the Continent, but that gave the Broome-Mister Softee combination a chance to consolidate—including David's success in the King's Cup just a few days after being bruised and battered by a heavy fall from Dr Pollard at the Great Yorkshire Show—and thus lay the foundations of a hugely successful partnership.

So, six years after David's first European Championship victory and five after Mister Softee's, with David Barker, the paired teamed up for a second success each in Rotterdam. The following year Broome also notched his second Olympic medal in Mexico, when he and Mister Softee finished third, after a jump-off, to Bill Steinkraus on Snowbound and Marion Coakes with Stroller.

So David and Mister Softee, after his usual winter holiday at his owner John Massarella's Yorkshire home, came to Hickstead in the summer of 1969 each in search of a third European gold medal.

Broome had deliberately not asked too much of Mister Softee in the lead-up to the championships, but Alwin Schockemöhle, generally rated his main rival for the title, could not have been in better form.

On the preceding weekend he had won the Hamburg Derby with his second string, Wimpel, while his main horse for the championships, Donald Rex, had been the best of Germany's bronze medal team in Mexico, and two weeks before Hickstead had won the International Championship in Aachen.

Second choice for Britain, rather than Harvey Smith, was Alan Oliver who, in contrast to Broome, had been in sparkling form around the national circuit. But he was not a regular on the Sussex showground, and that lack of experience told.

Broome and Mister Softee wasted no time in their defence of the title, and in the opening (speed) leg went round the 15-fence course so fast that even though they had to add five seconds for lowering a crossed pole were still fastest of all. Broome had Top of the Morning as his No 2, and underlined his mastery of Hickstead's international arena by taking third place on him, though only the best horse of each rider counted towards the championship.

Just as well for Schockemöhle that he had such a useful back-up as Wimpel, for while that horse took second place, 2.1sec behind Mister Softee, Donald Rex produced a unusually mulish display, stopped at the second part of the double, No 14, and dropped his rider. Schockemöhle quickly remounted and despite the mishap still finished seventh.

Alan Oliver's horses' inexperience of the arena played an even more crucial part: Sweep, with two fences down, was not too bad, coming in sixth, but Pitz Palu, the reigning British National Champion, also took a dislike to the 14th, stopped and slipped in to the first part,

OPPOSITE PAGE: David Broome and Mister Softee on their way to victory in the 1969 European Championship

an open ditch, and despite Oliver's attempts, after refusing twice more was eliminated there.

Hans Günter Winkler, the second German rider and a winner of four Olympic gold medals, took his Mexico horse Enigk round with careful precision, 14sec slower than Mister Softee but still into fourth place, ahead of the Swede Jan Olof Johannson (later to rename himself Wannius).

France's Pierre Jonquères d'Oriola had only one horse, Pomone, on which he won the 1966 World Championship in Buenos Aires, and when she ran out, also at the double, the 14th, his hopes were gone.

The course for the second leg of the championship was not too demanding, though the Italians Raimondo d'Inzeo and Vittorio Orlandi—neither with top horses—complained to the Technical Delegate that it was too big. It was certainly too much for Alan Oliver's horses. Pitz Palu was saved from a second elimination by being retired after two stops at the water, while Sweep had 20 faults in the first round and was retired in the second.

This left Broome to maintain the British defence alone. He and Top of the Morning went clear first time round, as did d'Oriola on Pomone, Winkler on Enigk and Schockemöhle with Donald Rex, but Mister Softee kicked down one of the poles over an open ditch.

He jumped clear second time, but now Top of the Morning made a couple of errors, while Pomone, Enigk and Donald Rex all repeated their first round zeros, to share first place.

The overall points took some working out, but it finally emerged that Schockemöhle had edged ahead, with Broome and Winkler sharing second. Had Oliver, even though he had no chance of winning, stayed in the contest, he might have been able to help Broome—as Harvey Smith did two years earlier—but now the Welshman had to do it all himself.

As if to make a point to the selectors, Smith took first and second places, on O'Malley (which he had taken over from David Barker) and Mattie Brown, in the day's other main competition, over a somewhat bigger course than the championship one.

The closeness of the top three placings meant that whomever of Broome, Schockemöhle or Winkler won the third and final leg, he would also win the championship. As usual, it was a two-rounder, run over 18 and then 12 fences, and being just behind the leader and needing to produce something extra special always seemed to bring out the best in Broome. So it was this time.

Time and faults in both rounds counted, and as Broome said later in his book *Jump-Off*, which he wrote with Genevieve Murphy: 'When Mister Softee is at his best I just have to sit on and steer him; he has a natural "flowing-on" style, is always very neat and careful and will do everything he can to avoid hitting a fence. In that last contest of the European Championships he was unbelievable; I even felt people were lucky to see him jumping, he was so rhythmic and economic, so ready and willing to jump his heart out.'

In the first round of that final leg the reigning champions were clear and fast, Donald Rex was also clear, but some three seconds slower.

Over the second, shorter (12-fence) course Mister Softee was even more impressive than first time, with a display of spectacular jumping which left the crowd breathless with admiration and excitement.

Schockemöhle took up the challenge, and Donald Rex was a fast horse; still in with a shout coming to the ninth, the treble, but they collected four faults there and another four at the next fence, dropping the great German rider to second—a place he seemed doomed to fill in perpetuity until the 'amateurs only' European Championship in 1975, followed by Olympic gold in Montreal a year later—with Broome claiming his third and final European title, a year before being crowned World Champion on Douglas Bunn's Beethoven.

Broome was the first rider ever to win the European Championship three times, and it was not done again until Alwin Schockemöhle's younger brother Paul completed a hat-trick in 1981, 1983—at Hickstead—and 1985 on his brilliant Deister.

OPPOSITE PAGE: The triumphant Irish lead the parade of teams after the 1971 European Junior Championships.

1971 – IRELAND AND SNOEK—JUNIOR CHAMPIONS

Juniors had their turn again in 1971 when a British squad that included Debbie Johnsey, who was to just miss out on a medal at the Montreal Olympics when she and Moxy finished third in a jump-off for silver and bronze, were expected to retain a title that had been won in St Moritz the previous year by a team that included John Francome, destined to become one of the greatest of all National Hunt jockeys.

But the only medal they managed was Rebecca Richardson's individual bronze on Relincho, behind Germany's Marion Snoek on Janeau and Ireland's future top international Paul Darragh with Woodpecker.

Marion, 18, whose brother Hendrik was a regular and successful member of Germany's senior squad and was the first from his country to win the British Jumping Derby, a year later, was a product of the excellent training of Germany's younger riders by Herbert Meyer.

Ireland and Germany also dominated the team championship: the two countries were equal on eight-fault totals after the two rounds—with Switzerland third on 12 and the British quartet a remote seventh of the 12 teams—and so had to jump-off for gold and silver.

The Irish had suffered a major setback when one of their horses, Bantam, owned by Lord Chief Justice Sir Robert Lowry, broke a leg when he kicked through the wall of his box only the night before the team championship, and had to be put down.

Kevin Barry and Costo, brought in as substitutes, clinched the Irish team victory when going clear in the jump-off, following equally faultless rounds from Charlie Curtis on Feltrim and Marilyn Dawson with Clare Cottage. Darragh and Woodpecker, who had jumped two clears already did not need to come out a third time. Four years later Darragh returned to Hickstead in triumph again when winning the Derby on Pele.

1973 – MCMAHON AND 'FORGIE' RULE THE ROOST

Fred Hartill bought hundreds of horses and ponies in his time, but never made a better bargain then when he paid £130 for Pennwood Forge Mill—'Forgie' to his many fans. He was Irish-bred, though no one ever discovered exactly what his breeding was, but with his proud Roman nose and strong physique, clearly Irish draught played a big part in it.

Hartill had show-jumped himself after the Second World War, and with his wife Valerie built up an increasingly busy dealing and schooling yard, which developed into a thriving riding school at Pennwood near Wolverhampton—hence the prefix given to so many of their horses—and Forge Mill was bought to be sold on.

Fortunately for all concerned, he was such a wayward character at first that he could not be put on the market, and by the time that he had settled down his potential was clear.

His early education with the patient John Wrathall, who took him up from novice to Grade A, played a huge part in his later, so-successful career. While still Grade C, in 1969, he paid his first visit to Hickstead, which was to be the scene, four years later, of the greatest of his many triumphs, in the European Championship, and by the end of 1970 he had qualified for the Horse of the Year Show.

Paddy McMahon took over the ride in 1971, and the partnership, which lasted until 1977, was one of accord from the start: on their first overseas trip together that season, to Ostend, they won the Grand Prix, the first of many wins in Britain and abroad that established them as among the best in the world, and 'Forgie' as a firm favourite with show jumping fans.

By coincidence, the manager of that British team in Ostend was Douglas Bunn, and there was another Hickstead connection, as Forge Mill's groom at that time was Sally Warren, whose father Bob was the Sussex ground's show director from 1967 to 1974.

McMahon had had considerable success with Tim II and Hideaway—who was to go to

OPPOSITE PAGE: Paddy McMahon and Pennwood Forge Mill are congratulated by HRH The Duke of Edinburgh after winning the 1973 European Men's Championship.

Alwin Schockemöhle on Weiler at the 1973 European Men's Championship

two Olympic Games with British teams; Munich, 1972, with Mike Saywell, and Montreal in 1976 with Graham Fletcher. Early in 1972 the question was whether Forge Mill would also go to Munich, but the selectors, in the end, decided against it in what was only his second international season.

In 1973, the horse was approaching his peak, which landed him European Championship, Horse & Hound Cup and King George V Gold Cup within the space of a week, but before all that he had to endure a journey—so vividly described in Sue Clarke's book *Forgie*—with the rest of the British team, to Madrid for the Spanish Nations Cup that could have put a less strong horse out for the season.

Boxed to Dunkirk, they went by train from there to the Spanish border in relative comfort, but then for the rest of the journey to Madrid were transferred to cattle trucks which were hitched behind a passenger train that went so fast it had the horses rocking on their feet. Some of the horses, though not Forge Mill, had to be given tranquillising injections by their grooms in pitch darkness at speeds up to 80mph.

On the way back they asked to be attached to a slower train, and were given one that took three days, in torrid heat, and then were left sitting on the French border for a day and a half. But in between, and despite all the travelling problems, McMahon and Forge Mill won three competitions, including the Grand Prix, and helped the British team win the Nations Cup.

None the worse, they arrived at Hickstead ready to take on the best in Europe for the 1973 title. Harvey Smith, who had been runner-up to Hartwig Steenken and Simona in the 1971 Europeans, in Aachen, as well as to David Broome in 1967 in Rotterdam, was the second British rider, with Hideaway and Salvador III.

They had 17 riders from 11 countries lined up against them, with Alwin Schockemöhle, second to David Broome four years earlier and still seeking his first major title, expected to

be among the most potent dangers, together with his compatriot Fritz Ligges.

McMahon and Pennwood Forge Mill began as they meant to, and indeed did, go on in the opening speed leg of the championships. The draw was not too kind to them, starting second of 31, but Paddy was not worried, saying: 'You've only got to do it once, and if we can go fast enough we can get them all worried.' And that is what they did, with an exhibition of jumping at speed round the 15 fences that none of their rivals could match.

Schockemöhle, whose Rex the Robber was his main hope, went first of all on his No.2, Weiler, also clear, in 91.6sec, a time Forge Mill cut by 0.9sec. Just as well Weiler had gone so well, as Rex the Robber had two fences down.

Smith and Hideaway had the equal fourth best time, but had to add 6sec for an error going in to the treble, which dropped them to 8th. Macken, who was to go so close to the World title 12 months later, was out from the start here, when Easter Parade stopped at the first and Oatfield Hills had three down.

Pam Carruthers set them all a tough task in the second, Nations Cup, competition, run during a torrential downpour, and the only clear in the two rounds came from Smith and Hideaway in the first. But four fences down in the second put paid to them, though Salvador made amends for Smith and was among six, including McMahon and Forge Mill, and Italy's Vittorio Orlandi with Fiorello, who finished equal runners-up.

Forge Mill's only first round error came at the treble, which caused a lot of trouble, but in the second he hit two, and the winner of the second leg was Frenchman Hubert Parot on Tic, who had also faulted at the treble in the first round, but had only an early error at a big oxer in the second. But his first leg score had left him so far behind that even this success did not pull Parot up beyond fifth place overall, while Schockemöhle's chance seemed gone when Rex the Robber had a fall at the water.

Consistency is the key to winning three-round championships, and that was always McMahon and Forge Mill's strong suit. Schockemöhle and Rex the Robber came back in brilliant style to win the third and final leg, but by finishing second—clear in the second round after, like his German rival, hitting one in the first—McMahon and Pennwood Forge Mill claimed the title by a clear margin. Schockemöhle climbed back up to second, just ahead of Parot and Orlandi.

On that same day, in an outside arena at Hickstead, Princess Anne and Doublet, on whom she had been crowned European three-day event champion two years earlier, won the Hickstead Combined Training (dressage and show jumping) Championship, just in time for the Princess to walk across to the international arena and see McMahon and his great partner's triumph.

Sue Bunn escorts HRH The Duke of Edinburgh to the Royal Box at the European Championships, 1973

Paul Schockemöhle with Deister after winning, in 1983, the second of their three consecutive European Championships

1983 – SCHOCKEMÖHLE AND DEISTER ON WAY TO HAT-TRICK

Ten years were to pass, and the rules changed so that men and women did battle together, and a team championship had been introduced, before Hickstead staged its next championship.

Alwin Schockemöhle had finally shed his 'perennial bridesmaid' tag in the 1975 European Championships—which, controversially were confined to amateur riders and were boycotted by the British, most of whose top riders had been made to turn professional—and followed up at the Montreal Olympics, but by the early 1980s it was his younger brother Paul who had taken over at the top.

Paul and his superb Deister won the 1981 European Championship in Munich, with Malcolm Pyrah and Towerlands Anglezarke second—which had earned Britain the right to stage the next championships—and in 1982 showed their liking for the Hickstead arena by winning the Derby, only the second from Germany to do so.

Schockemöhle, who was to do so much for Hickstead as a businessman in the years to come, and Deister underlined their affinity with the international arena there, and their current form, when winning the Grand Prix at the 1983 May meeting, although Paul was then still suffering some pain from a collarbone broken in March, and were still winning at the Aachen show just before the championships. Clearly they, and Germany as a team, were the ones to beat.

By contrast the British selectors had been having a difficult time as a result of various injuries and loss of form, and when the time came Pyrah and Anglezarke were the only combination of those originally chosen who actually made the line-up. Joining them were David Broome with Mr Ross, who had had back problems and a blood disorder, Harvey Smith on Sanyo Olympic Video and John Whitaker with Ryan's Son, who were only brought in to the side a week earlier, after an injury to Nick Skelton's St James.

Whitaker and Ryan's Son had lost what looked a certain place in the Montreal Olympic team seven years earlier when making a complete mess of the final trial, held at Hickstead, but that probably proved the best thing that ever happened to them. After that, among many other successes, they took individual and team silver medals at the 'Olympic substitute' meeting in Rotterdam (and were to win a proper Olympic team silver in Los Angeles in 1984).

The team contest, with 46 riders from 12 countries, turned into a marathon, with Walter Gabathuler on Beethoven (not, of course, Broome's 1970 World Champion), winning the opening speed round, ahead of compatriot Willi Melliger on Van Gogh, with Schockemöhle and Deister a close third, and eventually leading the Swiss team to their first success in the European Championships after near-misses in 1975 and 1981.

Britain's Ronnie Massarella was normally the most optimistic of team managers, often inspiring his squad to achieve more than they thought possible, but even he had not expected too much with his injury-hit side. For once he underestimated them: all four had one clear round apiece in the second, Nations Cup, leg of the team championship to keep up the pressure on the Swiss.

But they were equally consistent, with Thomas Fuchs on Willora Swiss and Heidi Robbiani on Jessica V, who were to win bronze in Los Angeles and silver in the 1985 Europeans, giving their team mates all the support they needed to clinch the title.

Germany had to settle for the team bronze, but individually Paul and Deister had gone in to a clear lead, from Gabathuler and Melliger, with seventh-placed Pyrah the best of the home side.

Schockemöhle and Deister needed only to keep their heads, and their accuracy, in the third and final round to win the championship—the middle leg of what was to be a unique hat-trick of European gold medals—and did so with aplomb, collecting only time-faults.

John Whitaker and his consistently successful Ryan's Son, silver medallists at the 1983 European Championships

By far the most impressive performance of the day came from John Whitaker and Ryan's Son with the only double clear that took them from ninth overnight into second place on the podium, ahead of France's Frederic Cottier and Flambeau C.

Whitaker, who had been desperately disappointed at originally being left out of the team, said: 'So when they put me in it, I just had to get on and do it.'

1999 – ALEXANDRA LEDERMANN THE FIRST

Although women were allowed in to the European Championships in 1975, it was not until 1999 that one finally won the title: France's Alexandra Ledermann on Rochet M. Both the individual and, especially, the team championships were among the closest ever, with Germany narrowly retaining the title they won two years earlier in Mannheim.

In the lead-up to the championships there had been much heated discussion about the ground in Hickstead's International Arena, Ludger Beerbaum having been particularly critical of it during the 1998 Nations Cup meeting. Germany had even walked out of the 1995 championships in St Gallen, Switzerland, because, they said, of the heavy ground.

Douglas Bunn insisted that the drainage that had been put in as part of the constant improvements always being made at Hickstead would ensure the going was perfect, but in the event this did not even need to be put to the test. The sun shone. Douglas's dream of making Hickstead the 'Glyndebourne of show jumping' took shape with renowned tenor Russell Watson performing at the colourful opening ceremony. The courses—by this time with Jon Doney as course designer—produced good exciting sport. As George Morris, trainer of the US team—who were, of course, not involved in the European Championships—said: 'It can't get better than this.'

There was a massive line-up for the championships, with 64 riders from 21 countries, 14 of them fielding full teams. Michel Robert, a veteran of the French team, who had competed in the three-day event at the Munich Olympics in 1972 and won team gold and individual bronze at the 1982 World Show Jumping Championships, scored in the opening leg, against the clock, on Auletto, with Sweden's Maria Gretzer second on Feliciano despite having an extra 5sec to add for hitting the final fence. But for that, she would have won.

Robert, 50, said afterwards that the course proved more difficult than he had expected. He was 12th to go, and said that had he started later and realised the problems: 'I would have been more careful, and slower.'

Marcus Ehning on the multiple Olympic gold medal winner For Pleasure was third ahead of the best of the British, Nick Skelton on Hopes Are High.

Germany were quite comfortably ahead of Sweden and Britain in the team placings, with Switzerland and Holland, the eventual silver and bronze medal winners, lying respectively sixth and fifth.

Everything tightened up in the deciding Nations Cup competition, when Geoff Billington and It's Otto raised the British game with a double clear round, though in the end the team had to settle for fourth.

After a contest that stretched all through the day, four teams were still in with winning chances with the last rider from each still to go. France were not among that quartet—they came in fifth—even though Ledermann and Rochet had boosted their individual placing by going round clear twice, and Robert with Auletto just kept the individual lead, with a clear and a four-fault round.

Their compatriots could not match them, but Meredith Michaels-Beerbaum—the first woman ever to ride in a German championship team—had better fortune when she also completed a double zero on Sprehe Stella. Ehning and For Pleasure also went clear second time, with Carsten-Otto Nagel and L'Eperon having just four faults. Meredith's brother-in-law, Ludger, on Champion du Lys, had a discard eight faults, but by then Germany had

OPPOSITE PAGE: Alexandra Ledermann, the first woman to win a mixed European Championship, on her gallant veteran Rochet M.

39

British-born Lesley McNaught with Duff, who took team silver and individual bronze for Switzerland in the 1999 European Championships

already won.

Thanks to their double clear in the Nations Cup leg, Alexandra Ledermann and Rochet M, who had won a bronze medal at the 1996 Olympic Games in Atlanta, went into the third and final leg of the Individual Championship lying a close fifth to compatriot Michel Robert. And when only they could go clear inside the time allowed in the first of the two rounds of the final, they surged in to the lead.

Ledermann, 30, a talented musician and linguist, had the oldest horse in the competition in the 16-year-old Rochet M, but there was nothing staid about their round, at a breathtaking pace and taking risks which paid off handsomely. Robert's Auletto and Michaels-Beerbaum's Sprehe Stella each had one fence down, plus fractional time-faults, but for Switzerland both Markus Fuchs on Tinka's Boy and British-born Lesley McNaught with Duff jumped clear—the only others apart from Alexandra to do so—with a half and one time-faults respectively.

They both climbed even higher when going clear second time round and were lying first and second when the French woman and her gallant veteran came in to the arena, last of all to go. They could afford to have one fence down and still win, and Rochet was showing no signs of age or the effects of his earlier exertions. But when they hit the fifth of the 10 fences, their safety margin had gone.

Ledermann had been riding Rochet M since the horse was nine, and had formed a marvellous, trusting alliance with him. She told us later that as the fence fell she said to herself: 'Oh my God, it's too early. But a stride later I told myself "OK, my horse is a fighter, we won't have any more down." He always gives everything when it is important.' They leaped the remainder of the course faultlessly, carrying Alexandra Ledermann in to the record books and creating another piece of show-jumping history at Hickstead.

Hickstead Jumping Championships – Results

1961 EUROPEAN JUNIORS
TEAMS: 1 Germany (R Buchholz's Chica; H von Zychlinski's Drossel; H von Opel's Cari; B Bagusat's Listo); 2 Holland; 3 Great Britain.
INDIVIDUAL: 1 S Barnes' Sola (GBR);
2 A Roger Smith's Fanshaw (GBR);
3 J Maslin's Arkvar (GBR).

1963 EUROPEAN WOMEN'S
INDIVIDUAL ONLY: 1 P Smythe's Flanagan/ Scorchin (GBR); 2 A Givaudan's Huipil/Caribe (BRA); 3 A Drummond-Hay's Merely-a-Monarch/O'Malley's Tango (GBR).

1965 WORLD WOMEN'S
INDIVIDUAL ONLY: 1 M Coakes' Stroller (GBR);
2 K Kusner's Untouchable (USA);
3 A Westwood's The Maverick (GBR).

1969 EUROPEAN MEN'S
INDIVIDUAL ONLY: 1 D Broome's Mister Softee/ Top of the Morning (GBR); 2 A Schockemöhle's Donald Rex/Wimpel (GER); 3 H G Winker's Enigk/Torphy (GER).

1971 EUROPEAN JUNIORS
TEAMS: 1 Ireland (C Curtis' Feltrim; M Dawson's Clare Cottage; K Barry's Costo; P Darragh's Woodpecker II); 2 Germany; 3 Switzerland.
INDIVIDUAL: 1 M Snoek's Janeau (GER);
2 P Darragh's Woodpecker II (IRL); 3 R Richardson's Relincho (GBR).

1973 EUROPEAN MEN'S
INDIVIDUAL ONLY: 1 P McMahon's Pennwood Forge Mill (GBR); 2 A Schockemöhle's Rex the Robber/ Weiler (GER); 3 H Parot's Tic/Port Royal (FRA).

1974 WORLD MEN'S
INDIVIDUAL ONLY: 1 H Steenken & Simona (GER); 2 E Macken & Pele (IRL); 3= H Simon & Lavendel (AUT) and F Chapot & Main Spring (USA).

1983 EUROPEAN (MIXED)
TEAMS: 1 Switzerland (W Gabathuler's Beethoven II; W Melliger's Van Gogh; T Fuchs' Willora Swiss; H Robbiani's Jessica V); 2 Great Britain; 3 Germany.
INDIVIDUAL: 1 P Schockemöhle's Deister (GER);
2 J Whitaker's Ryan's Son (GBR);
3 F Cottier's Flambeau C (FRA).

1999 EUROPEAN (MIXED)
TEAMS: 1 Germany (C-O Nagel's L'Eperon; M Michaels-Beerbaum's Sprehe Stella; M Ehning's For Pleasure; L Beerbaum's Champion du Lys); 2 Switzerland; 3 Holland.
INDIVIDUAL: 1 A Ledermann's Rochet M (FRA);
2 M Fuchs' Tinka's Boy (SUI);
3 L McNaught's Duff (SUI).

Alexandra Ledermann and Rochet M celebrate their gold medal in 1999.

Beethoven: Bunn's World Champion

'He had the mentality of a carthorse, but as soon as he left the ground he was magic.' – DAVID BROOME

Many riders and owners go their whole lives without having a really top class horse, but in one short 'shopping trip' to Northern Ireland Douglas Bunn bought two who were to prove among the best in the world—The Maverick and Beethoven. Quirky, perhaps, but with huge talent. Douglas had been invited by legendary horseman and dealer Jack Bamber to his yard in Ballymena, Co. Antrim to see The Maverick, who had already had some success in the show ring. Douglas had wanted just to buy the horse, unseen, but Jack insisted he went over to see him.

It was immediately quite clear that The Maverick was not exactly what Douglas was looking for, which was a big horse that was up to his weight, for The Maverick was a fairly lightly-built, athletic 15.3hh. He bought him anyway, and rode him reasonably successfully for a while, but it was in the hands of the much lighter Alison Westwood that The Maverick proved so brilliant, including winning the British Jumping Derby twice.

But tucked away in a corner of Bamber's yard was a horse who caught Douglas's eye. As he describes in Michael Clayton and Dick Tracey's *Hickstead: the first twelve years* Douglas asked: 'What's this black horse, he looks a big, powerful sort? Jack told me the horse had never been ridden, and was only a three-year-old. So we took the horse into Jack's barn, put up a rail at about four foot, and then shoo-ed the horse from one end of the barn to the other. He jumped the rail very well indeed, so I told Jack I'd buy the black as a travelling companion for The Maverick on the long journey from Northern Ireland back to Sussex.'

Douglas broke him in during the following February of 1962, and within weeks he was jumping fences up to 4ft 6in. Although Douglas was off for some time with a broken shoulder, after a fall from another horse, he qualified Beethoven for that year's final of the prestigious Foxhunter Championship at the Horse of the Year Show, in the Wembley Arena, and won it.

Son of Roi d'Egypte, out of an Irish draught mare, Beethoven was a quick learner, and the following season, when he was still only five, Douglas took him into international competitions. They were in the winning Nations Cup team at Ostend, a feat they repeated in 1964 and then in 1965, when they were also second behind German Olympic champion Hans Günter Winkler with Fortun, in the King George V Gold Cup. Only the two of them reached the timed jump-off, with dual Derby winners Seamus Hayes and Goodbye among those sharing third place. Touring the North American shows that autumn, Bunn and Beethoven won the Toronto Grand Prix.

It was a considerable achievement on Douglas's part to combine riding at the highest level with all his business interests and with running Hickstead, which was taking up an increasing amount of his time; but by 1968 the partnership was not going so well, and at the Surrey County Show on Whit Monday, 1968, came the changeover. David Broome, in the process of winning the main competition with Mister Softee, was sitting next to Douglas, who had been eliminated for three refusals. Not for the first time.

David asked Douglas if he would like him to have a ride on the horse, and the answer was 'I'd love you to.' David popped him over a few fences in the practice ring, liked the horse and Douglas suggested he might ride Beethoven in the next competiton. An immediate success it was not: no one but Douglas had ever ridden the horse in a competition, and Beethoven kicked, bucked, booted fences out of the way—but did finish. Douglas commented: 'Marvellous, that will do him the world of good.'

David took Beethoven round the domestic circuit, including winning at the Hickstead July meeting, but as he had three horses for the following week's Royal International Horse Show he suggested Douglas might take back the ride for that show. He did so, but after a promising start they had a crashing fall during the King's Cup, and for Douglas that was enough. Beethoven was David's ride from then on.

PAGE 60: David Broome and Beethoven safely off the controversial Irish Bank (as Douglas Bunn looks on)

David was delighted, for despite all of Beethoven's foibles he said at the time that he 'loved the horse. He is agile and clever as well as being big and strong. When he is actually in the air he is one of the nicest jumpers you could ever wish to see.'

Mister Softee was still David's top horse at that time. He had helped him win his second Olympic bronze medal in Mexico in 1968, but early in 1970 the horse's owner, John Massarella, sent David a letter telling him that he was keeping the horse at home, and that Malcolm Pyrah would be riding him. That combination did not work out, and 'Softee' went back to David, but he was an old horse by now—at least 18, maybe more. Owner and rider agreed that the World Championships in La Baule, especially with the controversial change-of-horse final, was out for him.

But if not Mister Softee, then who? He felt that Beethoven was too inconsistent, Ballywillwill had not the temperament, and Manhattan, the horse he was to ride in the 1972 Olympics in Munich, was too inexperienced. At the Royal Highland Show Beethoven was at his most uncooperative, and I well remember a despondent David telling me he wished he did not have to go to the World Championships.

The decision was made for him. The selectors had short-listed three riders to choose from: David, Harvey Smith and George Hobbs, but just days before the championships started George broke a wrist. David and Harvey it was, though the Welshman arrived in La Baule feeling he had little chance, and still had not finally decided whether to ride Beethoven or Top of the Morning. Douglas Bunn was in La Baule not just as an owner, but also as the British team's chef d'équipe, and after much consideration they opted for Beethoven. As David said, if the horse was in the mood they could certainly qualify for the final, and if not, they would probably be last. He felt that with Top of the Morning he could go quite well, but would have no hope of reaching the final.

The opening speed round was over a gigantic course. David said at the time he thought

TOP: Douglas Bunn and Beethoven after scoring a 'home win'
BOTTOM: Douglas Bunn and Beethoven stretch out over Hickstead's water jump, then an enormous 16 ft.

it the biggest Table C track he had ever seen; the heat in the French seaside resort was scorching; and David spent the whole morning suffering from a stomach upset. But he and the whole British camp were better by the end of the day, when Harvey on his dual Derby winner Mattie Brown emerged the winner and David was third, behind Alwin Schockemöhle on Donald Rex.

The German combination were the only ones in the entire competition to jump clear, but their time left them vulnerable and although both Mattie Brown and Beethoven dropped a foot in the water, their superior speed helped make amends.

In the second qualifier, run in two rounds over a Puissance course, Harvey and Mattie Brown ensured their place in the final when they were among only three to go clear twice. The other two were Italy's Graziano Mancinelli, who was to win a gold at the Munich Olympics on Fidux, and Hugo Arrambide of Argentina with the previous autumn's New York Grand Prix winner, Adagio. Harvey's overall lead was increased, but David and Beethoven dropped way back when having a fence down in the first round: only one, but with 10 going clear it pushed him back to seventh overall.

Something special was now needed, and David and Beethoven produced it, jumping the only double clear in the third and final qualifier to pull up to third overall, behind Harvey and Graziano Mancinelli, who had had to fight Fidux almost from start to finish but did so effectively. Schockemöhle, whose Donald Rex finished seventh in the third qualifier, was the fourth finalist.

This was the first time that two riders from the same country had ever qualified for a World Championship Final, but they had two nail-biting days to wait before it. And when it came, the course was a great deal bigger than they had expected, with a particularly demanding treble combination. Smith and Broome had been drawn to go third and fourth, with Mancinelli first and Schockemöhle second, each of them starting on their own horses.

Mattie Brown, so reliable hitherto, was the only one to have a fence down for his own rider, which cost them 5 ¼ faults instead of the normal four. When they all swapped horses for the first time Harvey had a tremendous struggle with Fidux, a surly, intractable German-bred who nearly carted his rider into the water jump, which was not being used, and, brought round sharply to the treble, hit the first element. But when David came to ride Fidux he looked a different horse: maybe his battle with Harvey had changed his view of riders, or maybe David had just, very quickly, found the key. Whatever the reason, they jumped round impeccably.

Beethoven might have been expected to help David by being difficult for the other riders. After David had ridden him clear, he said to himself: 'Now he's someone else's problem'; but, instead, the horse decided to play the game by all his riders. When Alwin Schockemöhle had him half a stride wrong at the treble combination, instead of stopping, as he so often had, he sailed through. As Bunn said to Broome: 'The rotten old devil, fancy him doing that!'

But a level playing field was enough for David. The only horse on which he had a fence down was Donald Rex, who crashed through the third element of the long treble, and with Mancinelli dropping into the water on both the British horses, that was good enough to make him the first, and so far still the only, British rider to win a show jumping world championship.

OPPOSITE PAGE: Douglas Bunn and Beethoven jumping in Rome's Piazza di Siena in 1966

The British Jumping Derby

'Douglas was the best man in the world at getting advertising, and that V-sign was a pretty good advert by him. He was a good man and we were the best of mates—it was only you press boys who made it seem otherwise.' – HARVEY SMITH

'We don't want to jump that!' was the widespread reaction among riders when in 1961 Douglas Bunn unveiled the 10ft 6in Derby Bank, which has since become something of an icon for the All England Jumping Course, but which was then regarded with great suspicion by riders accustomed to the flimsy poles that were the norm around the county circuit.

It was, of course, not just the Bank that brought a new dimension to British show jumping. The entire set-up at Hickstead had been designed to do just that: to give riders and their horses a chance to practise over the type of fence they needed to jump well if they were to hold their own in top international competition, and to put behind them the assertion that had been made some years earlier, at a show in France, that 'the British would do better riding bicycles than horses'.

At the beginning of 1961 one of the first features I wrote for *The Daily Telegraph* was about the need for 'match practice' over such fences, and in that case what I mentioned as being urgent was the ability to jump water. At the previous weekend's Hickstead meeting a 12ft water jump, which is certainly not too wide a distance and smaller than the one in Aachen, caused falls as well as faults; of 30 horses only one, Judy Shepherd (later Mrs Crago)'s talented Spring Fever, cleared it.

Douglas said at the time: 'The trouble is that the English are mostly just bad at jumping water.' And at a Continental show a horse who habitually faulted at the water was never going to be successful.

But at least the British were used to water jumps. The Bank was a different matter, and most of the riders, especially the more experienced ones, did not want to know. George Hobbs, a highly successful rider on the national circuit, and his brother Wally, who was a good friend of Douglas, were especially insistent that it was 'not real show jumping'. George, and David Broome, who five years later was happy to ride the great Mister Softee down the Bank, and won the Derby, were among those who refused to try it when the Bank was first used, at the meeting before the Derby, with horses coming down the less steep slope.

It was left to some of the younger women riders to lead the way. Alison Westwood, later Mrs Dawes, who was to win the Derby twice on The Maverick, was the first to try it, on Coady, which she bought from Douglas Bunn. The first winner of a competition in which the Bank was included, the Bristol Grand Prix, was Pat Moss (sister of Stirling Moss and herself a racing driver as well as a rider) on Geronimo.

A month later came the first running of the British Jumping Derby—sponsored as was the whole meeting by W.D. & H.O. Wills. And complain about the Bank though they did, prize-money of £1,275—which at that time was a British record—was enough to tempt no fewer than 60 starters, among them Broome with three horses, including the Argentine Olympic horse Discutido, who had won the Hamburg Derby and so was proven over a big bank.

But the British were all to play only minor roles behind Ireland's Seamus Hayes and Goodbye. Perhaps it was a happy omen for the future that the first Derby was won by one of the greatest show-jumping riders of all time, for the list of those who have followed him into the Hickstead winner's enclosure reads like a 'Who's Who' of the sport's élite.

Seamus Hayes had a career, in England and Ireland, that lasted through four decades and might have been even more notable had not his formative years been during the Second World War. Born in 1924 in Cork, Seamus moved to Dublin six years later when his father, Major-General Liam Hayes, was appointed Commanding Officer at the Army Equitation School at McKee Barracks.

As a lad he would listen outside the door as the great instructor Col. Paul Rodzianko, a Russian cavalry officer, trained the Army recruits, and he put what he had learned into action at an early age. His father bought him a grey pony called Snowstorm at Limerick Fair

PAGE 66: Captain John Ledingham and Kilbaha, winners of the British Jumping Derby in 1994 and 1995

in 1939, for £10, and over the next decade Snowstorm became one of the most valuable open show jumpers in the world, almost an Irish Stroller.

They won the Pony Championship at the Royal Dublin Society's Spring Show in 1943, and the following year won the Open Horse Championship there, beating Iris Kellett on Rusty, the horse on which she was to win the Queen Elizabeth II Cup at the Royal International Horse Show in 1949 and 1951.

Hayes and Snowstorm's partnership was interrupted twice when the grey was sold, first in Ireland and later to Yorkshire, but each time Snowstorm proved a disappointment until Seamus was asked to take over the ride. In Yorkshire they racked up no fewer than 25 wins in succession, including, after the pony had been bought by Tommy Makin, with whom Seamus was based for five years, winning just about every major championship on the domestic circuit.

Seamus Hayes was the Leading Rider in Britain in 1948, 1949 and 1951, but broke a leg in 1953 and was out of action for six months. After a successful year with the Massarellas in Yorkshire he set up his own yard in Northamptonshire, but during the winter of 1955-56 had another bad fall, which fractured his pelvis.

He was offered a job back where he started riding as a boy, as trainer of the Irish Army team at McKee Barracks, and took over there in January 1957. But he was unable to compete while doing that job, so after just over two years he retired from it, and returned to the ring, riding for Dublin-based Belgian businessman Omar van Landeghem, who was building up a strong string of Irish-bred horses. Within three months he showed he had lost none of his magic touch by winning the Dublin Grand Prix on Kilrush.

His success did not please everyone, and brought complaints that he should not be competing with the Irish team because he was a professional: they took some sorting out with the International Equestrian Federation, and although the FEI eventually decided

Alison Westwood and Coady, the first ever to go down the Derby Bank, in 1961

that he could continue to ride in Nations Cups, he was told he could not jump in Olympic Games. Two years later he joined Joe McGrath's stable—which was where, among other great horses, he joined up with Lady Jane Stanhope's Goodbye. They were to be mainstays of Ireland's Nations Cup teams for years to come, but Goodbye was only a six-year-old when Seamus Hayes arrived with him at Hickstead.

'HOW TO JUMP THE BLOODY BANK'

Douglas Bunn remembered it well: 'Seamus arrived the night before the first Derby, parked his lorry in a corner of the field and walked down to the ring, where a number of riders were looking at the fences. When somebody asked him what he was doing there, he replied "I've come to show you all how to jump the bloody Bank."'

The next day he did exactly that, and every other of the 15 daunting fences on that marathon 1,300-yard course as well, to notch the only clear round, with nine sharing second place on four faults.

As I wrote at the time: 'Along with a chorus of sighs of relief at reaching the finishing line in one piece, and still for the most part aboard their horses, came the realisation that the Jumping Derby, hard though it might be to win, was not the "killer course" that many of them had feared.'

In Michael Clayton and Dick Tracey's book *Hickstead; the first twelve years* Douglas gives a word picture of the course, fence by fence, and this could be an opportune place in which to repeat it because although the original site of the Bank was moved a short distance and the slope used in the Derby made slightly less steep, it has essentially remained the same:

'Fence one is easy—a big stone wall in the middle.

'The character of all the Derby fences is different from other classes, in that they are all very long, in some cases 30 or 40 feet, similar to the best three-day event fences.

'And fence two looks quite innocent, but in fact it's an oxer 4ft 3in high and 6ft wide.

'Fence three—two water ditches.

'Fence four—gate and rail.

'Five—a big wall.

'Six—an oxer which again is a very big fence, about 4ft 7in high and 6ft 2in wide; it is dead square and has a green hedge in the middle. It's a big fence you have to meet coming away from the collecting ring. On any course, a horse has most impulsion on turning at the top end of the course to come "home"; where he has least impulsion is turning away from the gate, going away. The biggest fence on the Derby course is met at that point where the horse is "going away".

'It was not originally planned that way, it just happened. I'd like to think it was a stroke of genius, but it wasn't. However, it is a very good test of the ability of horse and rider. When you have big spreads, opaque fences always make a horse back off more than a fence you can see through.

'After that oxer, the seventh fence is the Road Jump.

'Eighth is the Derby Bank.

'Nine is the fence at the bottom of the Bank, two strides away from the base. This is intended to test whether the horse has landed properly from the Bank. In fact in Hamburg this fence is one stride away, and it's bigger.

'Overall, however, the British Derby is much tougher. But I decided to give a little more leeway at the bottom of the Bank because I had the impression in Hamburg that where you had horses coming off this very steep Bank you were just handing the class on a plate to the very small, nimble horse. I think when you are designing a course you should try to make things as equal as possible. You should give a 16.3 hands or 17 hands horse, like Goodbye, the same chance as a nimble little goat like Stroller, who is only 14.2. Big horses

OPPOSITE PAGE: Seamus Hayes and Goodbye head the line-up from Pat Smythe on Flanagan. Handing out the rosettes is Pat Owens, Hickstead's first show secretary and still a regular helper.

at Hamburg are generally in trouble when they come off the Bank, but if you give them the extra stride they have a better chance of clearing the next fence.

'After the Derby Bank at Hickstead comes the Devil's Dyke. In itself it is an original design, but similar fences with a sunken element in the middle were of course known on the Continent, and it has been a feature of some three-day event courses for years. At Hickstead I would say the Devil's Dyke is the bogey. So many horses hit the first element coming into the fence. This is because they are not looking what they are doing; they are looking at what is to come next, instead of concentrating on jumping the first 4ft 7in vertical rails.

'Sixteen feet of water is the next jump; this was the first full, Olympic-sized water jump provided as a permanent feature of a British course.

'Following the water, the horse next meets the post and rails jump at 5ft 3in. I found that fence on the Bagshot by-pass! I was driving along one night when I suddenly noticed a new fence they had put up by the side of the by-pass. I stopped the car, got out and measured the fence immediately; then I incorporated it into the Jumping Derby. It is a super looking fence and I'm glad to have come across it.

'Next is the big open ditch—7ft wide, with a 4ft 7in post and rails on the landing side.

'Balustrades follow, at 5ft. Then there is the in-and-out of two gates. Quite a lot of horses fault here, because it is a long way round the Derby and you must maintain your concentration.

'Finally, the last fence—a 40-foot long silver birch oxer, with a 4ft 7in by 6ft 3in spread.

'For a newcomer to the course, I still think the most challenging obstacle is the Derby Bank. Although, as I have pointed out earlier, I have done my best to make the course a fair test for big and small horses, it has been won by some notably small, active horses—Nelson Pessoa's Gran Geste, Anneli Drummond-Hay's Xanthos and of course Marion Mould's Stroller. I don't think it is peculiar to the Derby, but as show jumping has become more difficult it seems, except possibly for the Olympic Games, that the smaller horses are superior to the big ones. The smaller horses have more brains, they are more nimble, better balanced, and have a better power-to-weight ratio.'

Douglas's wish to make the Derby course as fair as possible for all types and sizes of horses was surely shown to have been fulfilled 12 months later when two from the opposite end of the make-and-shape syndrome jumped off for the top prize.

So difficult is it to jump clear round the Derby course that the competition has often been won by horses that faulted in the initial round, but in 1962 two of them were clear. Ireland's Tommy Wade came to the meeting with a very strong hand, for not only had he, temporarily, taken over the ride on Goodbye, but he also had his diminutive and powerful Dundrum, a part-bred Connemara who stood only about 15 hands high but could, and did, leap puissance walls towering above him.

The day before, it had looked as though Dundrum might have to miss the Derby, as he was led from the ring after breaking a blood vessel. But all was well on the morning of the Derby, and, going 37th of the 60-strong field, Wade and Dundrum jumped the first clear round.

For a long time it looked as though they might be the only ones, giving Ireland a second consecutive success, but with just a handful left to go, Pat Smythe, the undisputed queen of British show-jumping riders, and Flanagan put in an equally immaculate performance.

There might well have been a three-way fight, as Bill Steinkraus and Sinjon, who had won on the first two days of the meeting, including the Derby Trial, appeared also to have gone clear. But the judges decided that the horse had started to go down the Bank and then retreated, before he did come down, and so they were penalised for a refusal. This still left them third, and Steinkraus won the style prize, but only two were asked to go a second time, against the clock.

TOP LEFT: Looking down from the top of the Derby Bank: (left to right) John Whitaker, Duncan Inglis, Franke Sloothaak (partly obscuring Freddie Broome), Damien Charles, Maria Gretzer and Tim Stockda

TOP RIGHT: Ellen Whitaker, a prolific winner at Hickstead, pictured with Ladina B during the 2009 British Jumping Derby

BOTTOM (LEFT TO RIGHT): Guy Williams—a Hickstead regular and winner of the British Speed Derby in 2002 and 2004; Andrew Mizon safely negotiates the Bank in the 2007 Derby; Charlie Bunn presents the Liz Dudden Memorial Trophy to Trevor Breen, winner of the Bunn Leisure Speed Derby in 2009; Geoff Billington clears the last element of the Devil's Dyke on his way to victory i

Nelson Pessoa and Derby specialist Gran Geste are congratulated by Douglas Bunn after winning the first of two British Jumping Derbies, in 1963.

The course is always shortened for a jump-off, with the Derby Bank omitted. This time, galloping at speed, Dundrum soared over the water but clipped the fence that followed. So Pat could take her time in guiding Flanagan round clear, and although they were nearly four seconds slower they never looked in danger of having a jumping error.

The huge crowd, delighted with this success, had plenty to thrill them during the contest, but nothing more than when Mary Barnes, older sister of European Junior Champion Sheila, and Sudden leaped in one bound from the top of the Bank to the bottom. Somehow Sudden kept his feet, and somehow too Mary was still with him when he did so.

A year later Pat Smythe declined to defend her Derby title on Flanagan, as it came in the middle of the meeting that also included the European Women's Championship, which she was attempting to—and indeed did—win, for a third successive time.

PESSOA STARTS A TREND

Wade was among the riders, including also Seamus Hayes and Tommy Brennan, who broke the long-standing military monopoly of Ireland's Nations Cup team. Although he and Dundrum had been foiled of a Derby victory, one of the other 'ponies' was successful, in the absence of Pat and Flanagan. This was the Brazilian ace Nelson Pessoa's diminutive grey Gran Geste, who was bred in Brazil by a thoroughbred out of a small native mare.

Born in Rio de Janeiro in December 1935, Nelson ('Neco') Pessoa was a phenomenon: so successful that when he came to live in Europe the International Equestrian Federation (FEI) had to change their rules to prevent him winning too often. Not that it did! And his son Rodrigo, who has been even more successful internationally, made his first competitive appearance in a pony class as a nine-year-old at Hickstead.

Until Nelson Pessoa came on the scene, Brazilian show jumping was dominated by the

country's army officers, but his precocious talent soon earned him recognition. He was still only a junior when making his international début, with the Brazilian team in neighbouring Argentina, and there scored his first international victory.

Such was his obvious talent that as a 20-year-old he was chosen for the Brazilian team for the Olympic Games in 1956 in Stockholm. He and Relincho—like Gran Geste a small grey, but without quite that horse's brilliance—were placed 33rd of the 66 starters, beating both his compatriots, with the team only 10th.

But just a few weeks later, the Brazilians pulled off a major shock in the Aachen Nations Cup, beating the home side, which included two of their gold medal trio, with Pessoa and Relincho again the best of their team. Continuing their tour to the Royal International in London, they finished second to Great Britain.

For the next three years Nelson travelled from Brazil to tour the top European shows as part of his country's Nations Cup squad, but he realised that to fulfil all that he was capable of he needed to be based in Europe. In 1961 he moved to Switzerland, and subsequently to France. He now lives in Belgium.

He rode both his own horses and those belonging to compatriot and fellow-rider Arline Givaudan, and his 'raids' on smaller, supposedly domestic, shows in neighbouring countries, France, Holland, Germany, and rather longer trips to Britain, were so successful that the FEI brought in a rule limiting the number of 'foreign' riders who could compete at a show unless it adopted full international status. As this involved paying the FEI a fee it was not a universally popular move, but Pessoa was so successful at the highest level as well it had no noticeable effect on his progress.

In his first season in Europe he and Gran Geste won the Grands Prix in St Gallen, Switzerland, and in Brussels, as well as the puissance, for the Lonsdale Trophy, at the Royal International Horse Show. And he was soon showing his particular liking for Derbies.

He won the 1962 Hamburg Derby with Espartaco, after a three-horse jump-off against Raimondo d'Inzeo on two, his Rome Olympic gold medallist Posillipo and 1956 World Champion Merano, and returned there in 1963 to finish equal first on Espartaco and Gran Geste, who had the only two clear rounds.

This was just before they came to Hickstead for the British Jumping Derby, and with Pat Smythe and Flanagan giving it a miss rather than risking her potential hat-trick of European Championships, Pessoa went into the contest as a firm favourite.

But this time the marathon course bit harder than before. There was not a single clear from any of the 44 starters, although David Barker and Mister Softee were unlucky not to have one, for they were faultless over every fence, only to slip up on the flat when making a sharp turn.

Four of the 44 reached the finish with just one mistake apiece—Gran Geste's coming at the smallest fence on the course, the 3ft 3in upright on top of the Derby Bank—and had to jump-off. This time Pessoa and his grey got it right all the way round, but Anneli Drummond-Hay and Merely-a-Monarch had two down and were beaten for second place by Pat Pharazyn with Sugar Daddy. Sheila Barnes and Sola, winners of the European Junior Championship at Hickstead two years earlier, retired into fourth.

If there had been an award for bravery it would undoubtedly have gone to Ted Edgar. He had badly injured his left arm in a schooling accident the week before, but rode Jacapo (who would be brother-in-law David Broome's Olympic mount in Tokyo) with the arm plastered and in a sling, and collected only eight faults. He much appreciated his special prize of Champagne and cigars, and the huge applause from the delighted crowd.

Pessoa won the Jumping Derby Trophy, a silver-gilt horse, but did not receive it as it had been stolen from a shop window in London's Piccadilly. At the presentation he had to settle for a photograph of it. But the brilliant Brazilian—whose compatriot and stable-mate

Arline Givaudan took the silver medal in the European Women's Championship which ended the next day—was to have a long and happy connection with Hickstead.

He and Gran Geste scored a second Derby victory two years later, when, with no initial clears, the two with four faults jumped off; this time Gran Geste made no mistakes, to win from Diana Conolly-Carew, Ireland's top woman rider at the time, on Barrymore. A half time-fault to add to four for jumping left Kathy Kusner and Untouchable third, while Harvey Smith might have started his run of Derby wins earlier than he eventually did (in 1970) had Warpaint, who jumped round clear, not pecked on the Bank and sent his rider 'out of the front door.' That did not happen too often.

However, Pessoa saved the best for last. Towards the end of a career that brought him a European Championship, in 1965—when not one of the medal winners came from Europe, which brought about another FEI rule change—a record-breaking seven victories in the Hamburg Derby, two gold medals and a silver in the Pan American Games, two World Cup silver medals, and over 150 grands prix, Neco returned to Hickstead in 1996 to win the British Jumping Derby for a third time, 31 years after his second success, on Loro Piana Vivaldi.

By now he was 60 years old—by a long way the oldest rider to win the Derby—and Vivaldi, which he described at the time as his 'best ever' horse, was aged 19. The previous November, Pessoa had had a heart attack, and so he rode the Derby course wearing a special watch that monitored his heart rate. It was the first thing he looked at after completing his round, but he had had plenty to test the condition of his heart earlier that year when his son Rodrigo, 14 years after making his competitive debut as a nine-year-old at Hickstead, had led the Brazilian team, which Nelson trained, to win the country's first ever Olympic equestrian medal by finishing third in Atlanta.

Pessoa senior said: 'Watching that was worse. When you are riding you can forget the pressure, but the Olympics was a good test for my heart. It showed me I could go on riding.'

No one went clear in the 1996 Derby, but Vivaldi faulted only going in to the Devil's Dyke, and seven shared second place on eight faults. Vivaldi, wearing a new bitless bridle because, said his rider, 'he is getting older and needs to be ridden lighter', and with such brittle feet that his shoes often dropped off, galloped straight down the Bank, but never looked like stopping at the upright at the bottom of it. Apart from at the Dyke, he produced a round that had a capacity crowd enthralled.

To say that the victory was an emotional one would be understating the case—Douglas said it was 'One of the best days of my life'—and the reward was greater, too. Pessoa's first two Derby wins had been worth £200 each, but in 1996 he collected a cheque for £40,000, and completed a record in Jumping Derbies that is unlikely ever to be bettered.

Goodbye and Seamus Hayes, with whom he was now re-united, returned to score a second success in 1964. They were taken to a jump-off by Marion Coakes (later Mrs Mould) and her pony Stroller, a combination that became firm favourites at Hickstead and in arenas around the world, and were more than adept at coping with Derby courses. They won the Hamburg Derby in 1970 and jumped clear at Hickstead three times. Although they only won the British Derby once, in 1967, they were second three times and third once.

Both Seamus on Goodbye and Marion with Stroller had to play second fiddle, along with five others, when David Broome and Mister Softee crowned a glorious 1966 season by jumping the only clear round to add the British Jumping Derby to the King George V Gold Cup, the British Olympic Trial and, later in the season, the Ronson Trophy, the Horse of the Year Show Championship. This was their first full season together, and it paved the way for much future glory, including the European Championships in 1967 and 1969 at Hickstead, under which chapter the full story of this tremendous partnership is told.

Because of swamp fever in 1966 the Irish were the only overseas riders able to compete

OPPOSITE PAGE: John Ledingham's Kilbaha, winner of the British Jumping Derby in 1994 and 1995 (on right) greets the 1996 winner, the 19-year-old Vivaldi, who gave Nelson Pessoa his third success at the age of 60.

ABOVE: The original British Jumping Derby Trophy which Eddie Macken won outright with four consecutive wins on Boomerang in 1976-79.
RIGHT: The Boomerang Trophy which Macken's sponsors, Carrolls, gave to replace it.

in Britain. Goodbye was among those who faulted at the Devil's Dyke, but both Diana Conolly-Carew on Barrymore, who had been runner-up the year before, and Marion with Stroller, got nearer to clear rounds, jumping the first 15 fences immaculately only to clip the huge silver birch oxer that finishes the course. The result, of course, was the same—four faults and a one-seventh share of second place.

MARION AND STROLLER AT LAST

Marion and Stroller, whose story, like that of David Broome and Mister Softee, is covered in more detail in the 'Championships' chapter, having claimed the Women's World title at Hickstead in 1965, finally had their British Jumping Derby triumph in 1967. There would have been little justice if they had not at some stage reaped the reward for their consistency around this unique track. Marion, who was 20 years, one month and 10 days, remains the youngest Derby winner.

Broome and Mister Softee won the Derby Trial, from Anneli Drummond-Hay on Merely-a-Monarch, with Marion and Stroller only seventh, but when it mattered most the gallant pony outjumped them all, with the sole clear round among the 44 starters. But it was a round that tested the nerves of their many supporters, not least Marion's father Ralph who was always her most enthusiastic helper. Marion told the story in full in Clayton and Tracey's account of Hickstead's first twelve years:

'My biggest worry was the last fence, the one we hit last year—a big rustic parallel, about 7ft wide, and it was a bogey I was not looking forward to right at the end of the course.

'Almost impudently, Stroller disposed of the other fences in the course which had caused trouble to his much larger competitors: the Devil's Dyke, a rustic treble of uprights leading in and out of a ditch, the 16ft of water, and the formidable double of gates. But, unexpectedly, we struck big trouble at Hickstead's famous 10ft 6in bank—a spectacular obstacle, with an almost vertical drop, yet one which does not usually cause much grief.

'Even so I do not think little Stroller cares for the bank, and I certainly share his opinion! Every year that we face the bank we seem to be even more frightened of it, but until this occasion we had not had any trouble there. As usual Stroller sprinted up the less-steep take-off side, hopped over the jump on top and then we faced that awful drop on the landing side. Halfway down poor Stroller stumbled and began to slither at an angle; all I could do was consciously 'do nothing'. In other words I left his head alone, which is just about the only policy to take on such occasions. Somehow, Stroller discovered a pony's 'fifth leg', miraculously saved himself from falling, arriving at the bottom of the bank in a perilous slide and a slither. It felt like an extremely bumpy toboggan ride on stilts! Yet despite all this, Stroller immediately recovered his poise and impulsion to be able to clear the next jump, a post and rails, which is only two short strides away from the bottom of the bank.

'Not at all abashed by his dramatic descent, which brought gasps from the edge of the arena, Stroller faced the remaining fences with confidence, and he put my fears at rest by soaring over my bogey fence at the end of the course, to finish the first clear-round that afternoon. It really was a wonderfully thrilling moment to leave the arena with the cheers of the crowd amounting to a roar.'

Alison Westwood, having been the first to show that the Bank held no fears for her when it was unveiled in 1961, had to wait seven years before she had her name inscribed on the British Jumping Derby roll of honour on The Maverick, which she had taken over when Douglas Bunn decided he was too heavy to do the little horse real justice.

He was not an easy horse. Douglas had broken a collarbone in a fall from him, and another rider had broken his back, but Alison suited him to perfection and they formed a long-lasting partnership which was still going strong when, with Alison now Mrs Mike Dawes and The Maverick sadly re-christened with the commercial name Mr Banbury, they

won a second British Derby in 1973.

Marion Coakes and Stroller's love affair with the Derby, which had earned them premier honours the year before, was as strong as ever and in 1968 they were clear again. But this time they were taken to a jump-off by Alison with The Maverick, who needed a prodigious jump to clear the palisades after the water when veering to his right, and produced it.

Seven years into its history, the Derby was already proving a huge public success. The 15,000 spectators were almost more than the stands could take, so that some of the more fearless among them even climbed the scaffolding of the television tower to get a good view. It was certainly worth the effort, and when the two women were sent round a second time, The Maverick set a furiously fast and faultless target that even Stroller could not quite manage. Marion knew she had to pull out all the stops, but when Stroller lowered the fence that The Maverick had so nearly hit first time round, he was retired into second place.

That was the year that David Broome took over the ride on Beethoven, on which two years later he won the World Championship in La Baule, from owner Douglas Bunn.

In July 1969 Alison with The Maverick and David with Beethoven teamed up with Anneli Drummond-Hay on Xanthos to win a three-horse relay at the prestigious Aachen Horse Show: not, perhaps, the most important of competitions, but something of an omen for the Derby.

> *'What has Hickstead done for show jumping? In England it has done everything. It started in 1960, the year I was born, so it has been going all my lifetime. I started riding here on 12.2s and (son) Jack has ridden here already, and he's only seven. It's been everything to me.'*
>
> MICHAEL WHITAKER

Xanthos, who was not a lot bigger than Stroller, had already proved himself a Derby horse in Italy, when the Rome International Horse Show moved for one day from its lovely setting in the Piazza di Siena to Olgiata, some 15 miles to the north. In the grounds of one of that country's most famous thoroughbred studs, where the great Ribot was bred, a tough course demanded a tough horse, and got it in Xanthos, who two days earlier had been in a scrap with David Broome's Ballywillwill, and still bore the wounds to prove it.

Clear first time round, he was taken to a jump-off by Germany's Hartwig Steenken on Porta Westfalica, but then beat him, living up to his nickname 'the little tiger'.

Xanthos had been back-up to Anneli's great horse Merely-a-Monarch when they won the European Championship in 1968, and again when just beaten for the title earlier in 1969 by Ireland's Iris Kellett with Morning Light. At Hickstead he was alone in the spotlight, with the only clear round over the demanding Derby course, beating Scotland's Aileen Ross and Trevarrion, who faulted only at the fourth fence, a gate.

That year it was not the Derby Bank but the much smaller Irish Bank (one of Hickstead's permanent obstacles but not included in the Derby course) which was the cause of much dissension among riders. Show-jumping horses are, of course, used to leaping fences in one go—obviously they cannot do this at the mammoth Derby Bank, but for the Irish Bank, at 5ft high, it could be possible. But they are intended, as in Ireland, to jump on it and off again, and the riders contended that it taught horses a bad habit, as they might try to do the same at, say, a thick bush oxer.

So when it was put in a competition the day before the Derby, a large number of them, including David Broome and Harvey Smith, refused to jump it, missed it out and were automatically disqualified, to the bewilderment of most of the spectators who had no idea

why this was going on. Marion Coakes was not among the 'strikers', and rode Daddy's Girl round without any problems at all, to win.

The issue of the Irish Bank rumbled on, and a couple of years later, in 1971, Broome again deliberately missed it out when riding Douglas Bunn's Beethoven—but both Broome and Bunn insisted there was nothing personal about it, and that it was just a matter of opinion.

HARVEY'S 'V SIGN' FURORE

What happened in that year's Derby, however, was a different matter entirely, brought a new phrase into the English vocabulary—the 'Harvey Smith sign'—and introduced Hickstead, and show jumping generally, to a whole new, and for the most part highly-amused, audience.

Harvey's victory on Mattie Brown in 1970 had been the third leg of a quick-fire hat-trick, which included also the Dublin Grand Prix and the King George V Gold Cup, all within less than three weeks. It was the first time Harvey had won any of them, and the first time any rider had won all three in the same season.

In the Derby they were taken to a jump-off by Alwin Schockemöhle and Donald Rex, but clinched the matter with a second clear. Schockemöhle had had a fall when his horse tried to bank the big oxer in the Derby Trial, and now had another at the same fence, even though the bush had been cut back, when going against the clock.

Twelve months later Harvey returned to Hickstead to defend his title, and was so confident of doing so that he had not brought the trophy with him when he arrived. Douglas insisted the trophy must be sent for, and Harvey did have it brought from Yorkshire in plenty of time for the presentation, but not before a good deal of needling had gone on.

Smith and Mattie Brown were certainly in top form for the Derby. They had helped

Harvey Smith and Mattie Brown—the winners of the British Jumping Derby in 1970 and 1971

Britain win the Nations Cup at Hickstead at the July meeting—a team which also included Steve Hadley and No Reply. In the Derby, Steve, now on Prospero, took Harvey to a jump-off; neither went clear, but Mattie Brown had a fence down going in to the Devil's Dyke, while Prospero had a refusal at the fence after the Bank, in those days for just three faults, plus one more for time. In the jump-off Mattie Brown had two fences down, but Prospero hit three, leaving Mattie Brown the first horse to win two British Derbies in succession.

All this was fairly routine, but not the aftermath, which I, along with most of the other press missed, as we had rushed off to write our stories: stories which had to be urgently re-written a couple of hours later, when we heard, while we were enjoying Douglas's hospitality at an after-show barbeque, that Harvey had been disqualified for making 'a disgusting gesture', and the first prize of £2,000—a world record at that time—had been forfeited.

As he galloped, victorious, through the finish line Harvey circled in front of the members' grandstand and directors' box, and made an elaborate, left-handed 'V' sign—

> *'The British Jumping Derby itself has become a national institution—it's one of those events a bit like the Grand National where it's not just the runners and riders that make the headlines but the course itself. It's an iconic showjumping contest, the like of which you won't find anywhere else in the world; no other course asks this much of a test of horse and rider and no other course creates this type of drama.'*
>
> CLARE BALDING

with his palm definitely facing inwards, not in the Churchillian 'V for victory' mode. It was recorded by BBC television, and though not used for their edited highlights that evening, was resurrected for the news programmes later, when the ensuing row broke out.

Two of the show's long-standing directors, the Hon. Janet Kidd and Mary Bates-Oldham, who was also a judge at the show, saw it and regarded it as a deliberate insult. Douglas did not see it live, but later saw a recording and agreed with them that it was an insulting gesture, completely in violation of Hickstead's rule on such behaviour, which stated that 'any act of discourtesy or disobedience to any Judge or Steward or any other Show Official on the part of an Exhibitor, groom or rider will entail disqualification, in which case...all prize-money won will be forfeited'.

Douglas missed seeing the gesture live because he was in the arena, where he presided over the presentation to Harvey. But when he heard about it later, after long discussions with Mrs Kidd and Mrs Bates-Oldham, he sent a telegram to Harvey, who had already left for his drive home to Yorkshire, telling him that 'because of your disgusting gesture, the directors and I have disqualified you'. They also decided that the £2,000 first prize should go instead to Steve Hadley.

Show jumping does not often make the front pages of national newspapers, but it did now—fuelled by the interest of those who saw it on the television news bulletins. Harvey, interviewed by a television reporter, insisted that: 'It was a straight forward V for Victory. Churchill used it during the war.' Douglas, similarly interviewed and asked whether withholding the prize-money could be justified, said: 'It is not a matter of the money. If it had happened in the smallest class in one of the outside rings exactly the same would happen.'

But three days later he agreed that he and the directors had been over-hasty in disqualifying Harvey without hearing his side. The prize-money was set aside, and the

matter referred to the British Show Jumping Association (BSJA), whose own rules on 'offensive behaviour' carried a possible 12 month suspension.

For well over a month the matter bubbled on, and it was a sign of how little hard news there was at the time that the press—and not just the equestrian press, though it made good copy for us too—and their readers gave it plenty of attention. The latter were fairly equally divided between those who supported Harvey's perceived tilt at officialdom and Douglas's stand against bad manners.

Douglas said later, 'I have watched standards and behaviour deteriorate in other sports, and my intention was to strike a blow for good manners'. Harvey insisted that he had not intended to cause offence.

When the stewards of the BSJA finally met to consider the matter at their London headquarters, there was another hurdle to overcome—they needed to see the film of the incident, and there was no projector to show it! They ordered one; ITN news sent for one of theirs—and the two arrived almost in a deadheat. For the door-stepping photographers and press this was more grist to their mill.

After much deliberation the stewards decided that although Harvey had made a gesture that 'he should have realised might have been considered offensive', they did not think he had contravened their rules on this matter. They also recommended that Hickstead should not withhold the prize-money.

A relieved Harvey Smith said he was happy with their decision: 'The gesture was not meant to be offensive—it was sheer excitement at winning. If Mr Bunn wants to come out and shake hands on the matter, I'm quite willing to do so.'

Douglas, still in the BSJA offices, was told of this, but felt some (less controversial) gesture was needed from Harvey. They met in the offices and minutes later the two men appeared together, announced that Harvey was going to donate £150 of the prize-money to Riding for the Disabled as his gesture of goodwill, and smilingly shook hands. That was the end of the matter as far as both men were concerned, though the 'Harvey Smith sign' lived on long afterwards.

Harvey, looking back on the incident 38 years later, said: 'Douglas was the best man in the world at getting advertising (for show jumping), and that V-sign was a pretty good advert by him. It was good for the whole sport, which certainly needs something like that now to shake the sport up a bit. He was a good man and we were the best of mates—it was only you press boys who made it seem otherwise.

'He was a generous host and had a great sense of humour. I remember we were having dinner at his house and, as usual, he was holding a conference. Threequarters of the way

The BBC's television cameras were the only ones to capture Harvey Smith celebrating his 1971 victory in his own unique style.

through the evening Banksie (the late Trevor Banks) rattled his glass, stood up and said "I'd like to propose a vote of thanks, to the most boring f-----r I've ever heard in my life." Then Bunnie rattled his glass, stood up and said "I'll second that!" That's the type of man he was, good and generous.

'Hickstead helped the international scene, and the British riders. He had the best horses in the world jumping there, and every English horse that went abroad, whatever fences it met there it had already jumped at Hickstead. He created team leaders, and now there are no team leaders. They are all just stooges and they've no character, nothing about them, and picking teams that aren't fit to go.'

Harvey went on to win the Derby twice more, on Salvador in 1974 and Sanyo Video in 1981, when he was standing in for his son Robert, who was under a month's suspension for 'misuse of the whip' at a show in Cardiff. They had the only clear round, and Harvey said afterwards: 'I have been telling Robert for three years that the horse could win (the Derby), so I had to show him how.' And to celebrate, after his winning round he dropped his reins, and gave a double-handed 'V sign'—to great applause from the crowd, including from Robert.

Robert has still yet to win the Derby, but his father is one of four to have triumphed four times, including also John and Michael Whitaker—who were jointly second to him in 1981—and Eddie Macken.

All of Macken's victories came on the same horse, the incomparable Boomerang, in succession in 1976-79, and he might well have made it five in a row, as Paul Darragh won in 1975 with Pele, a year after Macken had ridden Iris Kellett's horse into second place in the World Championship, at Hickstead.

Miss Kellett had changed riders when Macken, in order to further his show-jumping career, went to live in Germany in April 1975. Darragh, then 22, had won a few competitions in Ireland on Pele before attempting the Derby, but they nearly did not start as Iris was not convinced the horse was at his peak.

He needed to be, as the Derby developed into something of a slogging match on ground made heavy by torrential rain overnight. Tony Newbery and Snaffles also went clear, but in the jump-off they had four fences down. This should have made life easy for Darragh and Pele, but when they lowered three their supporters were holding their collective breath. Fortunately for them, that was all that fell.

Macken and Boomerang, who had already shown top form at the Royal International, Aachen and Dublin that season, won the 1975 Derby Trial only to have two fences down in the Derby, but a year later they started a run that will probably never be beaten. There are not too many horses like Boomerang nor too many riders with Macken's talent.

The son of a butcher in Granard, Macken once said he 'learned my sense of balance carrying sides of beef'. From almost the day he was born, Eddie's only interest was in riding horses. His father Jimmy was quoted, in Michael Slavin's marvellous book on Irish Showjumping Legends as saying: 'The stools in my butcher shop, the chairs at home, walls, whatever became horses and even then he rode them with style'. Given a cowboy suit for Christmas he galloped a farm pony up and down the main street firing his toy pistols—though when he tried the same thing with his local hunt he was, understandably, sent home.

So no wonder he left school early to spend as much time as possible riding horses, at first at the equestrian centre run by Brian and Ann Gormley and in 1969, at their recommendation, as a working pupil for Iris Kellett, who had seen him riding ponies at Ballsbridge.

A great rider and trainer, Iris Kellett later said of Eddie (and again I am quoting Michael Slavin's book): 'He came to me as a rough country boy but when he sat on a horse

OPPOSITE PAGE: Eddie Macken and Boomerang, who won the British Jumping Derby four times in succession, 1976-79

Michael Whitaker and Monsanta after completing a hat-trick of British Jumping Derby wins in 1993

it was magic—he had an excellent build, was supple, had the temperament and natural sensitivity. Above everything else, he had a feel for the horse.'

She worked him hard and taught him well, and he learned fast. Within 18 months of joining her yard Eddie was chosen for the Irish team for the Aga Khan Trophy, their own historic Nations Cup at the Dublin Horse Show, and he was never left out of the side for the next 10 years. In 1971 he rode in Europe for the first time, in Ostend, where he on Oatfield Hills, Ned Campion with Garrai Eoin and Larry Kiely on Inis Cara gave Ireland a first victory in the Nations Cup there. More important for Macken, it gave him a taste for Continental jumping that was to lure him back to live there four years later.

This was a time when Ireland was producing great riders as well as horses, including also at Iris Kellett's yard Con Power, father of Grand National winning jockey Robert; but Macken, with the talented Kellett horses to ride, outshone them all.

His next big break—arguably the biggest of all—came when he moved to Germany, to Paul Schockemöhle's stable at Muhlen. There he was reunited with Boomerang, which he had ridden, but not really got on with, at Kellett's before the horse was sold to Schockemöhle.

When his then-best horse Easter Parade broke his back in a freak accident on his way back to Germany from the (cancelled) spring show at Hickstead in 1975, Paul said to him: 'Take my speed horse Boomerang for the time being, until you get something better.'

BOOMERANG KEEPS COMING BACK

It was a partnership that became legendary in show-jumping history, with Grand Prix successes all around Europe and at Ron and Marg Southern's famed Spruce Meadows, Calgary, International. Macken topped the World Rider Rankings in 1976, 1977 and 1978.

Among all those triumphs were the four Derby successes at Hickstead, two with clear rounds. In 1976 they had the only one, with never a semblance of a mistake: Macken rode Boomerang in a hackamore, a bitless bridle, but always with the utmost felicity and slide-rule accuracy. Though he could have had a fight on his hands. It seems almost absurd to say that Marion Coakes, given how successful she was at Hickstead, was unlucky there, but consider that she and Stroller went clear three times, yet only won the Derby once. Now, on Elizabeth Ann, she looked from the grandstand to have jumped round clear, for certainly they did not touch any fence. But they were an ominously long time appearing on top of the Bank, and it turned out that they had slipped up as they climbed the gentle slope to the top of it. This cost them eight faults which left them only equal fourth, behind Judy Crago on Bouncer and Nelson Pessoa on Moet & Chandon.

Twelve months later Macken's Derby domination was even more complete, as he finished first and second, on Boomerang and Kerrygold (the renamed Pele). Boomerang's bridle had broken the day before and maybe the new one was the cause, for after jumping faultlessly all the way to the last, his head then got lower and lower, and he hit it. So they were among five four-faulters who jumped off, and this time Macken and Boomerang, going first, set a target none of the others could match. Kerrygold, the only other clear, was not much slower, 86.2sec to the winner's 85.8, with Malcom Pyrah third on Law Court.

It says much for Boomerang's toughness as well as his ability that he was able to complete the British Jumping Derby hat-trick in 1978 just seven days after jumping in the final of the World Championships in Aachen when Macken, as he had at Hickstead in 1974, finished runner-up, to Gerd Wiltfang. Neither Macken nor Boomerang had a fence down in the change-of-horse finale to the championships, but Macken was 0.8sec over the time allowed on Johan Heins' Pandur, and the quarter of a fault for that cost him the title.

At Hickstead he and Boomerang continued their impeccable progress to notch the only clear round, and a year later the Irishman's domination was total. In the Derby Trial he finished first and second, on Carroll's Boomerang and Kerrygold (Pele), and two days later he and Boomerang became the first to win both Trial and Derby in the same year. They were last to go, at which time, on rain-soaked ground, the best score was eight faults: Boomerang just misjudged the Derby Rails after the water, but that was their only mistake, and it was enough to complete the unique four-timer.

WHITAKER REIGN BEGINS

No family has been more successful in British show jumping, or possibly anywhere in the world, than the Whitakers, whose influence continues to spread with the generations, so it is fitting that the two who have played the biggest part in that collective triumph, brothers John and Michael, are among the four four-time winners of the British Jumping Derby.

Michael set the ball rolling for them with Owen Gregory in 1980 when he was 20, just under four months older than record-holder Marion Coakes/Mould. In recent years two 18-year-olds came close to inheriting the 'youngest Derby winner' mantle, Ellen Whitaker, Michael's niece, in 2004, and Andrew Mizon in 2007.

Michael had to wait 11 years for his next success, but then rattled off three in succession on Lady Harris's great horse Monsanta. They were second, behind John on the incomparable Milton, in the 1989 European Championships after a ding-dong battle throughout, and won a team gold; but by 1991 Monsanta seemed to be feeling his age—which was either 16 or 17, no one knew for certain—when going so badly in that year's Europeans, in La Baule, just before Hickstead, that they did not even qualify for the final.

But something about Hickstead clearly brought a rejuvenation, and to the delight of the sun-drenched crowd they had the only clear round. Whitaker said that he was glad they had not had to jump-off, as the horse was feeling tired at the end of his round. Luckily for them

the only other to get round without jumping faults, Tina Cassan, who has so often gone well at Hickstead, on Treffer was 1.08sec over the three minutes allowed, for half a time-fault.

Clearly Monsanta did not need the sun to bring out the best in him, for the 1992 Derby turned into something of a war of attrition when heavy rain turned the arena into a mudbath. No one jumped clear, but Michael rode him with kid-glove accuracy and their sole mistake, at the 13th, an open ditch, was good enough. Monsanta pitched on his nose after clearing the last when, according to his rider, he sunk in to the ground 'up to his fetlocks'. Michael said that the effort of winning 'took more out of him (Monsanta) than the Barcelona Olympics'.

They could not have had a more distinguished trio sharing second place: brother John's Gammon, who had to wait another six years before he got his head in front; Nelson Pessoa with Vivaldi, who was to give him such a notable triumph in 1996—Gammon and Vivaldi had both already won the Hamburg Derby—and Joe Turi with Michael Bullman's Vital, who won the British Jumping Derby in 1990, just before Monsanta's run started.

Michael had said after winning in 1991 and 1992 that he was glad he did not have to jump-off, as Monsanta was feeling tired, but though his luck in this did not hold in 1993, the gallant veteran again delivered the goods when getting the better of a three-horse barrage. In perfect conditions, totally unlike those a year earlier, Australian Chris Chadwick on his 16-year-old Mr Midnight, France's Hervé Godignon with his stallion Prince d'Incoville and Whitaker with Monsanta all jumped clear.

> *'Hickstead is a massive part of British show jumping. It is very historic. We've videos and videos at home of all the top riders over the years winning the great classes, and it is what inspires you. I dreamed of riding in the main ring when I was at school. I have nothing but lovely thoughts and memories of Hickstead—it is a fantastic place.'*
>
> ELLEN WHITAKER

Chadwick, going first, was determined to give the others a tough target but clipped the big spread fence out of the penultimate double; Godignon and Prince d'Incoville, who had previously been third twice in the Derby, lowered the third fence, but were even faster, leaving Michael in something of a quandary—try to beat them for time, or go for a steady clear?

Michael said that even as he went through the start he was not sure which way to play it, but that 'after jumping the third, I decided to go for a clear.' The plan could have gone astray when they tapped the pole out of the Dyke, but everything stayed up and Monsanta's hat-trick was safe.

By contrast with his younger brother, all of John's four wins—one should say 'so far' for both of them—have come on different horses, with 21 years between first and last. Hickstead played an important part in the career of John's first Derby winner, Ryan's Son. He rode him to victory in 1983 after finishing among the joint runners-up in two of the previous three years—they were to be second twice more—and four weeks after taking individual and team silver medals at the European Championships, on this same showground.

John and the then 15-year-old Ryan's Son jumped the only clear round. Paul Schockemöhle and Deister, who had beaten them for the European title as well as winning the 1982 Derby, this time-faulted going into the Devil's Dyke, and were among the five who shared second place.

John had started riding Ryan's Son—whose big white face and even bigger feet made him so recognisable, and who was destined to become a huge public favourite—when the

horse was a five-year-old owned by Donald Oates. He was for sale, but the price was more than Donald Whitaker, John's father, could afford, so he asked Malcolm Barr, a highly successful businessman, who was looking for a horse for John to ride, if he was interested. He was. Ryan's Son became John's first top international horse, and Malcolm Barr's daughter Clare, who went as a working pupil to John's yard, became his wife in 1979.

Early in his career, when Ryan's Son was just eight, he was called up suddenly for a trial for the Montreal Olympics, to be held at Hickstead. But he was a horse who needed a thorough preparation, especially as a youngster, and in the trial he did just about everything possible, including refusing, to put the selectors off choosing him. It worked, and was probably the best thing that could have happened to him, as the huge Montreal courses, jumped in deep mud, might well have ended his career before it had properly begun.

Four years after Montreal, when most of the equestrian world boycotted the Moscow Olympics because of the Soviet invasion of Afghanistan, John and Ryan's Son were chosen for the Olympic-substitute in Rotterdam, and won individual and team silver medals. A year after their Derby victory, they earned a real Olympic silver medal with the team in Los Angeles.

But a career full of medals of all colours was to end in the saddest possible way when, in the 1987 Derby, Ryan's Son, now 19 but still fit and in form, crashed and fell at the second fence, landing on his head. He was able to walk out of the arena, but a couple of hours later, while the chastened crowd was wending its way home, came the announcement that Ryan's Son had collapsed and died in his box.

John has always been able to keep his best horses in top form long after most of their respective generations have retired, and his next two Derby winners, Gammon in 1998 and Welham two years later, made Ryan's Son's success at 15 look almost like that of a juvenile prodigy.

John Whitaker, who has won the British Jumping Derby four times on different horses, pictured during his latest success, in 2004, on Douglas Bunn's home-bred Buddy Bunn.

JOHN WHITAKER'S OLD-TIMERS

Gammon, at 21, was the oldest horse to have won the Derby, and Welham, who had already been retired from international competition, was only a year younger when he conquered Hickstead's marathon course.

Gammon had been second in the Derby three times—in 1996 with brother Michael in the saddle—and was now the regular partner of John's daughter Louise, who had ridden him into second place in the 1998 Queen Elizabeth II Cup at Hickstead. When she said she did not want to ride in that year's Derby, John took over, though the horse was only considered his second string to the much younger Heyman.

One of Gammon's seconds had been in 1995 behind John Ledingham when, for the second year in succession, the Irishman added the Derby on Kilbaha to the Speed Derby, which he won three times in a row—1993/4/5—on Castlepollard.

Ledingham, from a County Waterford family steeped in equestrian competition—his sister Christine also jumped internationally—had his first taste of overseas competition as a pony rider in Toronto in 1968, joined the Irish Army equitation school at McKee Barracks in 1977 and was for many years a stalwart of his country's international team as it emerged from a period in the doldrums to become again one of the best in the world.

He remains the only rider to have won the Derby and Speed Derby in the same year twice—indeed, Ben Maher is the only other rider to have done so once, in 2005—and Ledingham and Castlepollard are one of just two combinations to score a hat-trick in the Speed Derby. Their successes followed immediately after David Bowen had completed the same feat on Delsey, in 1990-92.

Bowen and Delsey, which he bought as a five-year-old in 1986 for just £1,450, could so easily have notched up a four-timer, as they were second to Joe Turi on Mill Ruby in the third renewal of the Speed Derby in 1989 before starting their victory run in 1990.

In 1994 Ledingham and his Irish Army-owned mount had the better of a Derby duel against the clock with US rider Katie Monahan-Prudent, on Partly Cloudy, and in 1995 it was Whitaker and Gammon's turn to be out-jumped, when they had one down, leaving Ledingham and Kilbaha needing only a clear to win, which they easily accomplished.

Three years later the same two riders and horses had a return match, when once again they alone jumped clear and went into a jump-off. Determined to give it his best shot, Whitaker, again drawn to go first in the timed duel, sent Gammon off at racing speed, was six seconds quicker than in 1995, but clipped the first element of the Dyke. So once again a clear would have been enough to give Kilbaha his third win and Ledingham—who also scored on Gabhran in 1984—a record-equalling fourth. But at the first fence, the simple Cornishman, Kilbaha slipped on take-off and hit it, and could never quite match Gammon's pace.

Whitaker would have had two to go against Ledingham in 1995 had Welham not hit the last fence in the first round, and 2000 was just his second, and final, appearance in the Derby. Retired from international competition, after a prolific campaign that included a momentous double in the Aachen Grand Prix and King George V Gold Cup in 1997, Welham had the Derby as his main aim for Millenium year.

He did not let his supporters or his rider down. In a hard-fought jump-off between the three who went clear he beat Tim Stockdale on Wiston Bridget—a marvellously game daughter of a Clydesdale mare—and the ex-US racehorse Lionel ridden by Rob Hoekstra.

That same day we heard that Paul Schockemöhle's superb Deister, who completed a hat-trick of European Championships, including at Hickstead in 1983, and the British Jumping Derbies of 1982 and 1986, had died at home, aged 29.

Deister's career, and life, might well have ended much earlier, for in July 1982 the horsebox in which he was travelling home from a show in Paris overturned. One of the

OPPOSITE PAGE: Peter Charles and Corrada, who completed a British Jumping Derby hat-trick in 2001-2003

horses in it was killed but Deister survived with just a cut above one eye.

In the first round of the 1982 Derby he hit the smallest fence on the course, the upright on top of the Derby Bank, but then had the best of an eight-horse jump-off to beat Hugo Simon with his World Cup winner Gladstone, Michael Whitaker on Disney Way and John with Ryan's Son.

Schockemöhle might have won the 1984 Derby with Deister as well but for a broken bridle in the jump-off, after hitting only the final fence first time round; and he swapped to Lorenzo to win in 1985. Deister's lead-up to the 1986 Derby was hardly the best preparation, as, after winning the first round of the World Championships in Aachen, he had fallen in the practice ring and then, understandably, had a refusal when taken into the arena a few moments later.

Back in an arena where he habitually went well, Deister gave Schockemöhle the only first-round clear: John on Ryan's Son and Michael with Owen Gregory, together with Harvey Smith's Shining Example and Irishman Kieran Rooney's Hyland Serpent, shared second after all had hit an element of the Devil's Dyke.

If John Whitaker's first three victories in the British Jumping Derby were more or less according to plan, the results of years of horsemastership as well as skill in the saddle, his fourth can best be described as accidental—at least until it came to the actual competition when, of course, his ability to persuade a horse to give of its best, no matter how brief the acquaintance, proved to be crucial.

Douglas Bunn has owned a number of horses who have won in his own showground, mostly notably of course the 1970 World Champion Beethoven, but until 2004 he had never had a winner that he had also bred. Until Buddy Bunn came along.

Buddy Bunn was the son of one of a batch of Welsh Cob mares that Douglas bought from Fred Broome senior, David's father, and until the end of 2003 the horse was ridden by Douglas's daughter Chloe. She won the British Speed Derby on her father's Citi Dancer, in 1999, the year that Dutch-born but British citizen Rob Hoekstra fulfilled a 20-year ambition to win the Derby. Twelve months earlier Hoekstra and Lionel, who had raced in the United States as a two-year-old, had been among three who went clear, only to be relegated to third in the jump-off, but now there was no need for one, as they alone were faultless.

Like her father before her, Chloe was studying law, and did not have enough time to do justice to Buddy Bunn's obvious ability, so William Funnell was asked to take over the ride. William, whose wife Pippa has won two European three-day event championships and the Rolex 'triple crown' of eventing, and has shown her liking for the Hickstead showground by her successes in the Eventing Grand Prix, was happy to do so, and looking forward to riding him in the Derby.

But on the Monday of Derby week William suffered a severe groin strain when riding a young horse at the Surrey County Show and was still in acute pain when the meeting started. This did not stop him giving Douglas his first ever home-bred winner when partnering Buddy Bunn to swoop late and ease past Geoff Luckett on the ill-fated GG Barock in the Alberta Canada Stakes.

William said afterwards that he felt he would 'need a cortisone injection' if he were to ride in the Derby, but in the end it was decided that even a pain-killer would not be the answer. So his long-standing ambition to win the Derby was postponed—though he was to make up for lost time soon afterwards, winning in 2006, 2008 and 2009—and John Whitaker was called in as substitute.

He rode the horse for the first time on the Saturday, and a day later produced not one but two of those rounds which have earned him such respect among his fellow riders, as well as the public. In doing so he foiled the effort of his highly-talented niece Ellen.

OPPOSITE PAGE: Nick Skelton and Apollo won the British Jumping Derby in 1988 and 1989, giving Skelton, winner in 1987 on J Nick, a third consecutive success.

Ben Maher and Alfredo II en route to success in the 2005 British Jumping Derby

Ellen, at 18 two years younger than her uncle Michael when he won the first of his four Derbies in 1980, was the first to go clear, on AK Locarno. With this brilliant horse she was to help Britain win a team bronze at the 2007 European Championships—along with John and Michael, plus South Africa-born David McPherson. But then John followed suit on Buddy Bunn to force a jump-off.

Ellen would have been the first female winner since Alison (Westwood) Dawes on The Maverick (aka Mr Banbury) in 1973 had she prevailed, but after their faultless initial circuit they made one slip, at the Derby Rails, and gave John a chance he clearly had no intention of missing. A second calm clear was needed, and duly produced.

John's son Robert was among the quartet who finished equal third, and it can surely only be a matter of time before both of the cousins add their names to the Derby roll of honour.

In the 2004 Speed Derby Guy Williams and the aptly-named Be Precise did what no other combination has done, and regained the Speed Derby title that they had won in 2002, with quadruple Derby winner Michael Whitaker triumphing in between.

Nick Skelton is among a sextet of riders who have won three British Jumping Derbies, though as a youngster his ambition would have veered more to winning the Epsom rather than the Hickstead Derby, or more likely still the Gold Cup at Cheltenham, for he was racing mad—a gene that has clearly passed, very successfully, to his sons Dan and Harry. But when he went as a raw 15-year-old to Ted and Liz Edgar's nearby Warwickshire yard, for help in schooling a pony, his career took a different turn.

The Edgars suggested to Nick's father, a chemist, that he should join them when he left school, and the following year, 1974, he did just that, setting him on a course that has made him one of the most successful show-jumping riders Britain has ever produced.

It was a career grounded in hard work, riding novice horses or some, like Maybe, who were just plain difficult. Skelton's ability and determination resulted in him and Maybe,

who had a reputation as a 'stopper', being chosen for Britain's team for the European Junior Championships in his first year at the Edgars, and coming back with a team silver.

Ted Edgar was a dealer as well as a rider, with a huge number of horses passing through his Warwickshire yard, and Nick was given the chance to ride many of them. Twelve months after his first team silver he added a second on O.K., who had come from Belgian dealer Francois Mathy, and went on to take the individual gold.

Nick made the transition from junior to senior teams in 1978, when chosen for his first Nations Cup, and hit the headlines in December that year by breaking Donald Beard and Swank's British High Jump record, 7ft 6 1/4in, that had lasted since 1937. In the same Olympia, London, arena Nick on the grey Lastic, at their third and last attempt cleared the sloping poles at 7ft 7 5/16in (2.32m)—a height that remains unbeaten in this country.

Though his relationship with Edgar was stormy throughout the 12 years he was with him, Nick's progress to the top of international jumping was inexorable: a team silver on Maybe at the 1980 'Olympic substitute' in Rotterdam, a clutch of gold, silver and bronze medals in World and European Championships, and World Cup success in 1995 on Dollar Girl, having just missed out on St James 10 years earlier.

Nick's career came to a sudden halt when in 2000 he broke his neck in a fall that seemed to spell the end of his competitive riding. But he came back in time to partner Arko III in the Athens Olympics, and went heart-breakingly close to a gold medal.

SKELTON NICKS THREE

His first of three consecutive triumphs—so nearly four—in the British Jumping Derby, in 1987, with the only clear on J Nick, was overshadowed by the fatal fall of Ryan's Son. Skelton was the first to commiserate with his friend and team-mate John Whitaker, and J Nick himself had to be put down after a freak accident at a show in France in May 1988.

But also in 1988 Skelton became the first rider to win the Derby with clear rounds in consecutive years when Apollo, who had been runner-up in 1984, triumphed with two fences in hand, as none of his rivals got round for less than eight faults. Skelton took a chance with Apollo who always seemed to find the Devil's Dyke difficult, and instead of trying to ride it with slide-rule accuracy decided to 'treat it like a speed competition, gallop at it and hope he came back to me.' It worked perfectly. No fewer than seven shared second place, including Hungarian-born former circus trick-rider Joe Turi on both Vital and Kruger.

Joe and Kruger were sole runners-up 12 months later when Nick completed his hat-trick of victories, though this had looked unlikely when, on the opening day of the meeting, Apollo hit a pole during a practice jump and was hopping lame. Fortunately it

'Hickstead put British show jumping on the map. It was a great invention of Duggie's from the beginning. The main arena, and the fences, are unique, different from what you get in Europe or around the world. It is a very daunting ring. You need a brave horse that doesn't spook or look at things: horses like St James or Apollo. When you have won a big class in the main arena you've really achieved something. It has been a very lucky place for me over the years. When you've had two weeks of sunshine beforehand and Edward (Bunn) has watered it, it is the best ground in the world. Okay, when it rains it deteriorates a bit, but I think a lot of horses have got soft, been spoiled by the all-weather surfaces. I still prefer jumping on grass to anything else.

NICK SKELTON

turned out to be no worse than a knocked nerve, and the horse was fine again when it mattered. But after winning twice with the only clear rounds, Skelton had a fight on his hands, with both Kruger and Philip Heffer's Viewpoint also faultless.

In the jump-off Kruger went first and fast, but stopped at the Dyke and then hit the last, though he was quick enough to have no time-faults. This time Apollo also lowered the final fence so that Philip and Viewpoint, winners of the Swedish Derby at Falsterbo two weeks earlier, needed only a clear. But an error coming out of the Dyke and a foot in the water relegated them to third.

After two near-misses, Joe Turi certainly deserved the change of luck he had on Vital in 1990, but Nick and Apollo, in search of a hat-trick, took them to the wire. Vital, a stallion, had not been in a competition for a month as he was covering mares at the Oxfordshire stud of Michael Bullman, with whom Turi had been based for most of the time he lived in England after refusing to return to Hungary and seeking asylum. Penniless and unable to speak English, Joe performed miracles to reach the top of the show-jumping ladder in England: alas, when he did return to Hungary, after the end of communism there, he was killed in a motorcycle accident.

Vital needed all his pent-up energy when, after an immaculate circuit of the Derby course, he was forced to a jump-off by Nick and Apollo, whose headstrong round nevertheless made him the first horse to jump clear three times since Marion Coakes's Stroller.

In 1989 Vital had lost a place in the jump-off when hitting the final fence, and now, racing against the clock, he clouted the same fence. Joe said: 'I thought that would mean we'd be beaten again. But it was so hot he could hardly stand up afterwards.'

Apollo, aged 15 (four years older than Vital) felt the heat even more, hit the third fence, a gate, and then retired after also lowering the rails after the water.

The hat-trick that Apollo so narrowly missed did fall to Peter Charles and Corrada, in 2001-03. Liverpool-born Peter Charles rode successfully for Britain during the early part of his international career, and now does so again, but in 1992 he opted for his parents' country and changed to the green jacket of Ireland.

Peter, a pupil of both Iris Kellett and Eddie Macken, rode for Ireland in the Barcelona and Atlanta Olympics, and was in the Irish team that won the European Championship in 2001 on Corrada. But it was Carnavelly, on which he won the Derby Trial, that he thought his best chance of success lay in the 2001 Derby, as he was worried about how Corrada would come down the Bank. So worried, indeed, that he was concentrating more on the prospect of that than on getting her through the start on time. He started three seconds late and finished, without jumping faults, two seconds over the time allowed. He thus became the first rider to win both the Derby Trial and the British Jumping Derby at the same meeting on two different horses.

Charles' compatriot Billy Twomey, in his first Derby, on Give Me Remus, and Nicky Boulter with the hard-pulling Magna Carta shared second place with one fence down apiece.

The clock was not kind to the Irish in that Derby, as Kevin Babington and Carling King, also members of the championship gold medal team, started too early, before the bell had rung, and were automatically disqualified.

Although Peter's worries about Corrada's ability to come smoothly down the 10ft 6in Bank proved unfounded in 2001, a year later they were certainly justified when she took off halfway down, did amazingly well to not collapse in a heap at the bottom, but threw her rider so far forward that his hat was over his eyes.

Peter said later: 'I couldn't see a thing, I had to leave it to her.' But the gallant grey mare measured the fence at the foot of the Bank, and everything else, to perfection.

OPPOSITE PAGE: Douglas Bunn and Dame Vera Lynn, the Vice-Patron of Hickstead, present William Funnell with the British Jumping Derby trophy in 2008.

THE DFS DERBY
HORSE
dfs

She had to do it all over again—over a shortened course, without the Bank—as Robert Smith and Mr Springfield, the Derby Trial winners, had already gone clear, but in the jump-off Mr Springfield hit two and Corrada was clear, thus relegating Robert Smith to second spot for a fourth time.

If their first two Derby winning performances had flaws, there were none when Peter and Corrada, now 14, completed their hat-trick. It was as good a round as has been jumped over this always demanding course, every fence being cleared in a perfect rhythm.

Peter said in admiration after completing the only clear of the competition: 'I'll never have a horse jump the Derby course as easily as she did. All I had to do was to keep cool, get the strides right and leave it to her. She does things her own way, but there was never a danger she would have a fence down.'

Until they came into the packed arena Michael Whitaker was within sight of a unique fifth Derby victory, after Ashley had hit only the fence at the bottom of the Bank. It was the first time that season that Michael had ridden his mare, having lent her to Geoff Billington's son James to take in the European Junior Championships, in which they jumped a double clear.

'The Bunns have been great mates for a long time, and I'm godmother to Georgia, one of Lizzie (Bunn)'s daughters. If it was not for the shows, I suppose we would never have met them. The showground has done an awful lot for the Funnells—it is a fantastic place to produce young horses. You just don't get other shows like it. And (maybe I shouldn't say this) but it is a real social venue too. Much as I love jumping here, I also love coming here for a day off, to support William and catch up with people.'

PIPPA FUNNELL

William Funnell and Cortaflex Mondriaan, that season's Swedish Derby winners, would have added a £50,000 bonus had they also won at Hickstead, but two elements of the Devil's Dyke down left them only third. William, whose turn was not far away, had been unlucky not to have his name on the Derby roll of honour already, in 1997, when John Popely and Bluebird won with a four-fault round.

Comex, who had been suffering from a corn on his off-fore, pulled a shoe off that foot when clearing the Dyke and, perhaps feeling the pain, stopped at the 13th, the Open Ditch. William said: 'I think he was very brave to carry on'. Three faults for the refusal would still have been enough for victory, but Comex, also a Swedish Derby winner, had clipped the small upright on top of the Bank, which left them only second.

John Popely, who did not start show jumping until he was 16, 13 years earlier, was making his sixth Derby appearance, and Bluebird her fifth—never for less than eight faults—so were not winning out of turn. Their only mistake came when jumping out of the Devil's Dyke.

When John Whitaker rode Buddy Bunn to victory over his niece Ellen in 2004, Ben Maher and Alfredo missed joining them in the jump-off by slightly misjudging the time, and collecting one fault, for third place.

But Ben, so unlucky not to be among the medals at the 2008 Olympic Games in Hong Kong, when Rolette ran out of steam in the final round, only had to wait a year for his Derby consolation, at the main expense of Tim Stockdale who also could so easily have come home from the Beijing Games with a medal.

None went clear in the 2005 Derby, though Tim nearly did so on Fresh Direct Cloudy Night, who was still without fault coming to the last. Stockdale, realising how close he was

to making the same error as Maher 12 months earlier and getting a time-fault, pushed on to the final oxer and hit it.

As it turned out, a time-fault or two, or even three, would still have earned them first prize, as only Ben with Alfredo could even match their four-fault circuit, hitting the middle of the Devil's Dyke. Alfredo was not a horse who liked to be hurried, so trainer Steven Smith advised Ben to let him jump round at his own pace, saying: 'If Tim was faster, then we would have to hold our hands up and say we got it wrong.' But it proved the right recipe, as Cloudy Night hit the third fence and Tim retired into second place.

Ben, who at 22 was the youngest winner of the Derby since 20-year-old Michael Whitaker 25 years earlier, was only the second rider, after John Ledingham (twice), to add the Derby to the Speed Derby, which he won on Mercurius.

After his near-misses, and losing the winning ride on Buddy Bunn through injury, William Funnell had a deserved change of luck in 2006—which improvement in fortune was underlined with two more successes in 2008 and 2009, all on Julie Slade's Cortaflex Mondriaan.

William, whose wife Pippa 'farmed' the early runnings of the Eventing Grand Prix to add to her many triumphs in more formal three-day events, was 17 when he first rode in the Derby and 40 when he won for the first time, so no one could say it was not his turn.

A farmer's son who came up through the Pony Club, William had a choice of farming or show jumping as a career, and when, at 16 and having left school, he was offered a job as second stable rider to Simon Trent at Cyril Light's Brendon Stud, the die was cast. Within six months Simon left and William was promoted, became British Young Rider Champion, was third in the European Junior Championships and had his first taste of the rigours of the demanding British Jumping Derby course.

Through the intervening years he has shown his ability to get the best out of a variety of horses, including the talented but sometimes recalcitrant mare Amber du Montois, which he took over successfully after such master horsemen as John Whitaker and Peter Charles had tried their hands.

Comex, on which he was runner-up in the 1997 British Jumping Derby, was among the first of the series of horses he has partnered in Nations Cup teams, but it was on Mondriaan that he made his championship début, in the 2005 Europeans when the injury-hit team could finish only sixth.

FUNNELL'S LONG WAIT ENDS

William and Mondriaan showed that they meant business at the 2006 Derby meeting when winning the Trial, beating Robert Smith on Jerry Maguire in a two-horse jump-off, before going on to claim the prize he most wanted two days later.

Mondriaan was out of action for five months during the early part of 2006 after having a colic operation, and came into the competition a fresher horse than most of his rivals, which probably helped during the sweltering heat that prevailed throughout.

No one went clear initially, so the three with four faults had to jump-off. They were led by South African-born David McPherson—who was to contribute to Britain's bronze medal at the 2007 European Championships—on Bob's Diamond, which had been third in the Trial with the fastest four faults. They were fast again, but faulted again, at the big Privet hedge. Then Geoff Billington on Cassabachus had two down in chasing their time.

So William had to make the difficult decision: to try and match McPherson and Bob's Diamond for speed, or rely on Mondriaan's usually accurate jumping. He chose the latter course, and Mondriaan did not let him down, so that they became the first since Eddie Macken and Boomerang in 1979 to win both Trial and Derby in the same year.

Geoff Billington had been in the international doldrums after the retirement of his

great horse It's Otto, a team bronze medal winner in the 1997 European Championships and the Worlds a year later and unlucky not to get an individual medal in the Atlanta Olympics, but he has recently made something of a comeback.

Lady Rowallan's Cassabachus played a leading role in this, and after finishing third to Mondriaan in 2006 put things right the following season, on ground soaked by four inches of rain in one day. The drainage system proved well up to the job, although the course had to be modified, as outside the arena all was a sea of mud. Cassabachus produced a round of immaculate jumping, marred merely by one time-fault. Geoff said: 'It means everything. Last year it was my fault he had a fence down and I knew he could do it.'

In the process he spoiled what would have been a tremendous result for 18-year-old Lancastrian Andrew Mizon, who with Special Diamond led until Geoff's round, after hitting only the upright at the foot of the Derby Bank. But Mizon was happy enough with second place, saying: 'If it wasn't for Geoff, I wouldn't be here.'

Andrew's father, Richard, is a dentist and Geoff one of his patients. Just three weeks earlier Geoff had suggested to Richard that Andrew, who had had a successful career in pony and junior jumping, should ride Special Diamond in the DFS Derby. Although the entries had closed, Geoff persuaded the Hickstead management to give him a late entry, so it would have been an unkind fate had Andrew beaten him to the winner's enclosure.

After waiting so long for his first Derby victory, William Funnell rattled off three in four years. In 2008, he and Mondriaan came up against Geoff Billington with Cassabachus in a timed duel after, again, there were no initial clears and only the two of them finished on four-fault totals. This time Funnell and Mondriaan had to go first, not last as in 2006. Once again William opted for a steady clear, in the hope that Cassabachus, would prove fallible, as he had in the Derby Trial when he hit four fences. And again William's gamble paid off: Cassabachus hit the same fence, the Derby rails, as he had in the first round.

Also in 2008 Shane Breen became the first husband to follow his wife, Chloe (née Bunn, who triumphed in 1999 on Citi Dancer) into the winner's enclosure after the Speed Derby, in a record time, 91.96sec, on Royal Concorde. 12 months later it stayed in the family when Shane's younger brother, Trevor, won on Adventure de Kannan.

William Funnell and Julie Slade's now 15-year-old Mondriaan returned for a third victory in 2009, and this was their best performance of the three, a round of magnificent control and accuracy. It came after a somewhat fraught lead-up, when they tripped up on the Bank in the Hamburg Derby a few weeks earlier. William was propelled out of the saddle, and Mondriaan then trod on him, luckily without too much hurt to either of them.

When they came into the Hickstead arena, last of the 30 to go, the massed spectators still awaited a clear round: the joint leaders on four faults were Guy Williams with Skip Two Ramiro and William Whitaker on Animation, who, respectively, had hit the first and last elements of the Devil's Dyke.

In both of their previous successes Mondriaan had also faulted going into the Dyke in the first round, before clearing it in the jump-off, so William devised a 'cunning plan' to avoid that this time. He had surmised that since a sharp turn into the fence seemed to suit Mondriaan better than a straight-forward approach, running on from the upright at the foot of the Derby Bank, he would take a devious route around the Road Jump and approach the Dyke at an angle.

It worked to perfection, though William said afterwards that he was sure Mondriaan would have jumped clear whichever route he had taken. Mondriaan never looked in the least danger of hitting anything, and his rider said: 'He's a fantastic horse, and I go in to the ring with such confidence on him. I was a little worried about the Bank, after Hamburg, and last year I had to coax him down it, but this time he just took me through

OPPOSITE PAGE: Shane Breen on Royal Concorde in the 2008 Bunn Leisure Speed Derby, which he won in a record time of 91.96 seconds

HICKSTEAD

Partners in crime: William Funnell (left) and Geoff Billington share a joke whilst walking the course.

it. He's done so much for me, since winning the Foxhunter Final, and he feels better than ever.'

This was the 50th clear round of the British Jumping Derby, and the huge crowd gave them a standing ovation, but, despite the brilliant blue sky, a dark cloud hovered over the 2009 Derby meeting, for only 12 days earlier Douglas Bunn had died. The show went on, of course, as Douglas would have insisted, with riders past and present and many other old friends assembled before his funeral, which was held the following day. Riders in the Derby wore black armbands, and William summed it up for all of them when he said, after the presentation: 'I had very mixed emotions when I looked up at the (directors') box, and there was no Douglas.'

The British Jumping Derby, above all else at Hickstead, is his living memorial.

> *'Douglas Bunn was undoubtedly the greatest innovator in British show jumping in the post-war years. He succeeded in creating his personal vision virtually on his doorstep and he made the horse world come to him in his native Sussex. Douglas had flair, originality in making horse sports fun for the spectator and offered a new challenge to the competitor. He relished controversy, and was never afraid to break new ground. His contribution was unique, and he will be much missed by his many friends. Above all he was a true horseman, and loved the challenge of cross-country riding in the hunting field as much as the disciplines of show jumping.'*
>
> MICHAEL CLAYTON

David Broome: a Personal View

Winner of the 1970 World Championship on Douglas Bunn's Beethoven and a regular winner at Hickstead from its earliest days

Douglas created his own empire, but everyone benefited from it. He started Hickstead at the most opportune time, when show jumping was really big, and he did it in a style that suited Douglas. Relaxed but stubborn, that was his style. He would not have his main ring over-used and he had fences that were unique in the world, and every one of them was different: unlike so many fences that go on a lorry from one show to another and are all much of a muchness. That difference, the gates, the walls, the ditches, the banks, is what makes Hickstead unique, but it is also what causes some of the riders' resistance. It always has.

The main ring at Hickstead was Douglas's shop window and he wanted it always to look its best. The fences were always gleaming. You would not believe the amount of paint that was used on them—if a little chip came off you could see the paint was a quarter of an inch thick. He set a very high standard. And, very important, he always worked hard at getting the crowds there. It was the place to go, and it still is.

Douglas provided me with a world champion in Beethoven, at La Baule in 1970, and a year earlier Hickstead was the stage for perhaps the greatest moment of my career. In the final of the 1969 European Championship we had to jump two rounds against the clock, and Mister Softee was unbelievable. It was pressure jumping at its most intense, but he took the pressure you gave and rose to the occasion. I don't think he ever got the credit he deserved for his performance at the Mexico Olympics in 1968, when he had two of only four rounds inside the time, but his performance at Hickstead the following year was, I thought, just out of this world.

For the best part of 50 years we lived with Hickstead, and we lived with Douglas, bless him! It has been a wonderful journey, and great for show jumping. I think that what he has done for the sport will only be realised in the years to come.

David Broome and Mister Softee receive the Ben O'Meara Trophy from Douglas Bunn after their victory in the Hickstead Derby Trial in 1967, following their victory in the 1966 British Jumping Derby.

British Jumping Derby – Winners

1961 Seamus Hayes with Goodbye (Ireland)
1962 Pat Smythe with Flanagan (GB)
1963 Nelson Pessoa with Gran Geste (Brazil)
1964 Seamus Hayes with Goodbye (Ireland)
1965 Nelson Pessoa with Gran Geste (Brazil)
1966 David Broome with Mister Softee (GB)
1967 Marion Coakes with Stroller (GB)
1968 Alison Westwood with The Maverick VII (GB)
1969 Anneli Drummond-Hay with Xanthos (GB)
1970 Harvey Smith with Mattie Brown (GB)
1971 Harvey Smith with Mattie Brown (GB)
1972 Hendrik Snoek with Shirokko (Germany)
1973 Alison Dawes (Westwood) with Mr Banbury (The Maverick VII) (GB)
1974 Harvey Smith with Salvador (GB)
1975 Paul Darragh with Pele (Ireland)
1976 Eddie Macken with Boomerang (Ireland)
1977 Eddie Macken with Boomerang (Ireland)
1978 Eddie Macken with Boomerang (Ireland)
1979 Eddie Macken with Boomerang (Ireland)
1980 Michael Whitaker with Owen Gregory (GB)
1981 Harvey Smith with Sanyo Video (GB)
1982 Paul Schockemöhle with Deister (Germany)
1983 John Whitaker with Ryan's Son (GB)
1984 John Ledingham with Gabhran (Ireland)
1985 Paul Schockemöhle with Lorenzo (Germany)
1986 Paul Schockemöhle with Deister (Germany)
1987 Nick Skelton with J Nick (GB)
1988 Nick Skelton with Apollo (GB)
1989 Nick Skelton with Apollo (GB)
1990 Joe Turi with Vital (GB)
1991 Michael Whitaker with Monsanta (GB)
1992 Michael Whitaker with Monsanta (GB)
1993 Michael Whitaker with Monsanta (GB)
1994 John Ledingham with Kilbaha (Ireland)
1995 John Ledingham with Kilbaha (Ireland)
1996 Nelson Pessoa with Loro Piana Vivaldi (Brazil)
1997 John Popely with Bluebird (GB)
1998 John Whitaker with Gammon (GB)
1999 Rob Hoekstra with Lionel II (GB)
2000 John Whitaker with Virtual Village Welham (GB)
2001 Peter Charles with Corrada (Ireland)
2002 Peter Charles with Corrada (Ireland)
2003 Peter Charles with Corrada (Ireland)
2004 John Whitaker with Buddy Bunn (GB)
2005 Ben Maher with Alfredo (GB)
2006 William Funnell with Cortaflex Mondriaan (GB)
2007 Geoff Billington with Cassabachus (GB)
2008 William Funnell with Cortaflex Mondriaan (GB)
2009 William Funnell with Cortaflex Mondriaan (GB)

LEFT: The Band of the Royal Engineers provide a musical start to the Derby action. RIGHT: Trophies held high: supermodel Jodie Kidd (left) and Chloe Breen. Douglas Bunn was Jodie's godfather, and she is godmother to Chloe's daughter Lorna.

British Jumping Derby – Clear Rounds

1961 & 1964 Goodbye

1962 Flanagan

1962 Dundrum (Tommy Wade, Ireland)

1964, 1967 & 1968 Stroller

1966 Mr Softee

1968 & 1973 The Maverick (Mr Banbury)

1969 Xanthos

1970 Mattie Brown

1970 Donald Rex (Alwin Schockemöhle, Germany)

1974 Salvador

1974 Buttevant Boy (Graham Fletcher, GB)

1975 Pele

1975 Snaffles (Tony Newbery, GB)

1976 & 1978 Boomerang

1980 Owen Gregory

1981 Sanyo Video

1983 Ryan's Son

1986 Deister

1987 J Nick

1988, 1989 & 1990 Apollo

1989 Viewpoint (Philip Heffer, GB)

1989 Kruger (Joe Turi, GB)

1990 Vital

1991 & 1993 Monsanta

1993 Mr Midnight (Chris Chadwick, Australia)

1993 Prince d'Incoville (Hervé Godignon, France)

1994 Partly Cloudy (Katie Monahan Prudent, USA)

1994, 1995 & 1998 Kilbaha

1995 & 1998 Gammon

1999 & 2000 Lionel II

2000 Traxdata Wiston Bridget (Tim Stockdale, GB)

2000 Welham

2002 Mr Springfield (Robert Smith, GB)

2002 & 2003 Corrada

2004 Buddy Bunn

2004 AK Locarno (Ellen Whitaker, GB)

2009 Cortaflex Mondriaan (the 50th clear round)

British Speed Derby – Winners

1987 John Brown with G & A Castle Townsend (GB)

1988 Emma-Jane Mac with Everest Gringo (GB)

1989 Joe Turi with Mill Ruby (GB)

1990 David Bowen with Delsey (GB)

1991 David Bowen with Delsey (GB)

1992 David Bowen with Delsey (GB)

1993 John Ledingham with Castlepollard (Ireland)

1994 John Ledingham with Castlepollard (Ireland)

1995 John Ledingham with Castlepollard (Ireland)

1996 Michel Robert with Alligator Fontaine (France)

1997 Jane Annett with Pipakie (GB)

1998 John Renwick with Brookend Raphaella (GB)

1999 Chloe Bunn with Citi Dancer (GB)

2000 Billy Twomey with Sublime (Ireland)

2001 Jens Fredricson with RS Isaac (Sweden)

2002 Guy Williams with Be Precise (GB)

2003 Michael Whitaker with Dobels Frechdacks (GB)

2004 Guy Williams with Be Precise (GB)

2005 Ben Maher with Mercurius (GB)

2006 Ben Maher with Mercurius (GB)

2007 Ellen Whitaker with Henri de Herne (GB)

2008 Shane Breen with Royal Concorde (Ireland)*

2009 Trevor Breen with Adventure de Kannan (Ireland)

* In record time of 91.96 seconds

Pikeur
Pikeur
Pikeur
Pikeur

The Cups: King's, Queen's and Nations

'These riders have fulfilled a wonderful dream for me.

I'm sure my friend Douglas was looking down on us with a smile.'

– SÖNKE SÖNKSEN

The official records show that Hickstead staged its first Nations Cup in 1975, but that is far from the whole story, which begins four, or even five, years earlier.

In December 1969, at their annual general meeting in Brussels, the International Equestrian Federation had brought in a new rule governing the number of riders who could compete at CSIOs, the official shows each country is allowed to hold that include a Nations Cup. If more than four countries took part, the host country was only allowed four extra riders in addition to their 'official' squad of six.

There had been a potential difficulty early in 1971 when the British were told that they could send only five riders, with 10 horses, to the French CSIO at Fontainebleau. As the British squad were due to go on to France after competing in Rome, and the Italian squad contained six riders and 12 horses the manager, Douglas Bunn as it happened, would have had to drop one rider and two horses. So the BSJA said they would by-pass the French show altogether.

As the Rome squad included David Broome and Harvey Smith, who had finished first and third in the previous year's World Championships, in La Baule, as well as Mike Saywell, who won the Grand Prix at that meeting, the French had second thoughts and decided to let all six ride.

In Britain, show jumping, enormously popular and with big audiences for the BBC's televised programmes, was in a state of flux. Since the Royal International Horse Show, which has its origin in Olympia, London, in 1907, was reopened after the Second World War in 1946, the Nations Cup had always been held outdoors, at first in the marvellously atmospheric White City Stadium and, when that was closed, in the Wembley Stadium, which was really too vast to give the occasion the intimacy it needed.

After the 1969 show it was clear that changes were due. It was decided to keep the showing classes in the stadium but to have the jumping in the adjacent indoor Empire Pool. Even then it was hinted that the Nations Cup might go to Hickstead, but early in 1970 the show organisers decided that all the jumping should be in the Empire Pool, including the Nations Cup.

It worked well enough, but Colonel Mike Ansell, who ruled British show jumping in those days, always felt that the Cup should be held outdoors. So it was decided to split the show in 1971, with the Nations Cup, for the historic Edward Prince of Wales Cup, as the principal competition in a four-day meeting at Hickstead, followed, after a rest day, by the Royal International, including the classic King George V and the Queen Elizabeth II Cups, in Wembley's Empire Pool.

But, as the time for the joint-show approached, it was clear that, with seven countries apart from Britain planning to send teams, the British would only be able to have a total of 10 riders at their own international, even in the vast open spaces of Hickstead's All England Jumping Course.

Mike Ansell was quite prepared to limit the number of British riders to those who had been in teams at Official Internationals, or had won Area International Trials, but that still came to 21 riders, more than double the allowed number. Said Ansell: 'Is it fair to ask a rider to jump for Britain abroad and then refuse to let him compete at his own international?'

NATIONS CUP 'UNOFFICIAL'

Unless the FEI relented, he said, the RIHS would relinquish its 'official' label and just be an ordinary international show. And that is what happened. Hickstead ran its first Nations Cup and the British team won. It was the team's first Nations Cup victory of the

PAGE 106: German chef d'équipe Sönke Sönksen and the victorious 2009 Meydan Nations Cup team (left to right): Janne Friederike Meyer, Andreas Knippling, Max Kühner and Rebecca Golasch
OPPOSITE PAGE: British chef d'équipe Ronnie Massarella holding the historic Edward Prince of Wales Cup after the team's success in the 1971 'unofficial' Nations Cup. On the right are the Earl of Westmorland and John Wilson, chairman of sponsors W.D. and H.O. Wills. Holding the tray of rosettes is Hickstead Show director Bob Warren.

Molly Ashe-Cawley, twice winner of the Queen Elizabeth II Cup (in 2004 and 2006)

season, after disappointments in Rome, Fontainebleau and Aachen. As far as the FEI was concerned, it did not count, but the thrilled 20,000 spectators cared not a jot as Steve Hadley on No Reply, Graham Fletcher with his Aachen Grand Prix winner Buttevant Boy, and dual Derby winners Alison Westwood on The Maverick and Harvey Smith with Mattie Brown edged home by just one fence from Germany, with the United States third.

Strangely, after such a successful initiation at Hickstead, the Nations Cup then returned indoors to the Empire Pool for the next three years, but that was long enough, and in 1975 the 1971 formula was repeated, the show being staged at the same two venues, Hickstead and the Wembley Arena. This time there was no problem about the number of British riders who could take part, and the Nations Cup has been held at Hickstead every year since, except in 1997.

Hickstead has had more than its fair share of financial crises, usually bailed out by Douglas Bunn himself, but in 1997 the showground's future looked in grave and immediate danger after Silk Cut, who had sponsored the All England Jumping Course for 16 years, withdrew their funding, of £400,000 annually.

Douglas appealed to the Sports Council for help from the National Lottery fund, with little response. He said at the time: 'I asked the (Sports) Council for a life-raft from the National Lottery to save the season because Hickstead is a national asset and they have money specifically for sport. But I got nowhere. They said they might give me £100,000, but they never made me a firm offer. In any case I would still have to find £600,000 from my own funds.'

As a result of this the Prince of Wales Nations Cup was held as part of the Royal Windsor Horse Show, and there were fears that the whole year's programme at Hickstead, which by now included the Royal International Horse Show as well as the British Jumping Derby, might be lost. Luckily these fears were quickly allayed when Paul Schockemöhle,

who had such success as a rider there and was by now a hugely-successful businessman, and show organiser, used his marketing company to help ensure that the show could go on, and, with Douglas's own contacts, the necessary sponsorship was found.

That first official Prince of Wales Cup at Hickstead in 1975 could not have been more thrilling. Although seven countries had sent teams, the British were hot favourites to win, with a team that, as in 1971, included Harvey Smith and Graham Fletcher, and now also David Broome and Paddy McMahon. All four had proven track records over the Sussex showground, whereas Germany, who looked likely to be their main rivals and were leading in the President's Cup—the season-long Nations Cup Championship inaugurated by Prince Philip, the then-President of the FEI—had a very mixed team.

The Germans were preparing for that season's European Championships in Munich—which were for 'amateurs' only and were to be boycotted by the British. Their Hickstead team included two very experienced riders, Alwin Schockemöhle—who went on to win individual and team golds at the European Championships—and Hendrik Snoek, plus two first-timers, Hans Quellen, a pupil of Schockemöhle, and Hendrik Schulze-Siehoff.

The Dutch and Australians, who were on a European tour, both fielded only three-rider teams: Paul Weier was a late defector from the Swiss squad and the Belgians had a sub-standard side.

IRISH PUT UP A FIGHT

But the Irish made sure it was not a two-sided contest, and after the first round were equal first with Britain. Both Michael Hickey on Nordel and Ned Campion with the brave and consistent mare Garrai Eoin were clear and it was only a mistake at the water—by, of all horses, Eddie Macken's Boomerang—that prevented them being in the lead.

Schockemöhle on Rex the Robber and Snoek with Rasputin both had double clears, but their compatriots could not quite match them. Smith and Salvador were the only British combination to get round twice without fault, but Broome with Heatwave, in his first Nations Cup, and McMahon with Pennwood Forge Mill, the 1973 European Champions, each had one clear. Fletcher, who had to change to Tauna Dora when his Aachen Grand Prix winner Buttevant Boy developed sinus trouble, had only one fence down each time, and in the tightest possible ending the British won by just one time-fault from Germany, with Ireland third, four faults behind the winners.

It was a contest that augured well for the future of the Prince of Wales Cup in Hickstead's spacious International Arena, and also for the British team, who were on the verge of a golden era. That the experience the British riders and horses gained at Hickstead contributed to that success is undeniable.

Germany gained their revenge a year later, when the Nations Cup was held as early as April because of the upcoming Olympic Games in Montreal. It was again a close contest, but hardly one with any bearing on the Olympics, which were still confined to 'amateur' riders. Three of the four British riders, Harvey Smith, David Broome and Malcolm Pyrah, were all, therefore, ineligible for Montreal, with only Debbie Johnsey, on Moxy, as a potential for the Games. Debbie and Moxy did, indeed, make it. They failed only by the narrowest margin to win an individual medal, when third in a jump-off for the silver and bronze behind Alwin Schockemöhle.

After that came a run of four straight successes for the British team at Hickstead, a period that was perhaps most significant for John Whitaker's establishment as an important, often crucial, member of the team—a state of play which continues until this day.

The spread of Whitaker family talent is now so wide that the very idea of a major team without one or more of them in it is almost unthinkable. John was the first, making his Nations Cup debut in 1975. He and Ryan's Son were in such brilliant form in the early

part of 1976 they seemed sure to be chosen for the Olympics, until, at a hastily-arranged final trial, at Hickstead, they 'bombed out'.

Ryan's Son, then just eight years old, stopped so many times that the selectors had no option but to drop him. I, to my subsequent shame, wrote in *The Daily Telegraph* that the trial had 'lit up the limitations of Ryan's Son' which John's brilliance in the saddle had hitherto 'kept in the shadows'. This about a horse which was to be the mainstay of the British team for years to come, including individual and team silvers at the Olympic 'substitute' meeting in Rotterdam in 1980, and a real team silver in Los Angeles four years later. The problem in fact was that Ryan's Son always needed to be prepared for a show, and he was rushed into this one because there was not enough prior warning that it would happen.

RYAN'S SON IN WINNING DEBUT

John and Ryan's Son, who returned to Hickstead later in the season to win the National Championship, made their Prince of Wales Nations Cup debut the following year. The team did not need to be at its best to coast to a comfortable victory over the Dutch—that year's European Champions by a quarter of a fault from Britain—in a high-scoring competition by 19 faults to 35.

Twelve months later there was an even easier, and much more significant home victory, when the British team, Derek Ricketts on Hydrophane Coldstream and David Broome with Philco, both of whom jumped double clears, and Caroline Bradley with Tigre and Malcolm Pyrah on Law Court, who each had a clear and a four-fault round, sauntered home on a zero fault total, with runners-up the United States collecting 20 faults.

The same British quartet went on just over a week later to take the World Team Championship in Aachen, Germany, and the team was unchanged, except that David rode Queensway Big Q, when completing the Prince of Wales Cup hat-trick in 1979.

Surely it was an indication of the depth that British show jumping then had that the four-timer was completed in 1980 with an entirely different side: John Whitaker and Ryan's Son were recalled, together with Robert Smith on Video, Lionel Dunning with Jungle Bunny and Liz Edgar on Forever, on which she was, that season, the first woman rider ever to win the Aachen Grand Prix—first run in 1925—as well as the Grand Prix at Hickstead.

1980 was a momentous year for Hickstead, as W.D. & H.O. Wills, after being the sole sponsors since the showground opened 20 years earlier, announced that they were discontinuing their sponsorship. Douglas had often said that without their support Hickstead would never have got off the ground, but now added that he was looking forward to the future and to Hickstead growing even more.

Douglas was right to be confident, though the next 30 years were to bring logistical and financial problems, highlighted by the 1997 transfer of the Nations Cup to Windsor. Throughout its history Hickstead has been among the top-ranked shows worldwide, and when the International Equestrian Federation introduced the Samsung Super League in 2003 it was among the eight showgrounds selected to stage these most prestigious of Nations Cups.

The Super League, which lasted until 2008, consisted of the eight top national teams worldwide contesting these eight shows. They were all in Europe, as Ron and Marg Southern's marvellous show at Spruce Meadows, Calgary, which would surely have been among them, opted out so that they could invite whichever teams they wanted. With their rich prize-money they had no worries about teams failing to turn up.

The idea of a super league was surely a good one if show jumping was to retain, or should that read 'regain', media attention at a time when almost all sports felt the need to accommodate spectators' apparent decreasing attention span. Quicker is better—vide

LEFT: Janne Friederike Meyer and Cellagon Lambrasco who jumped three clear rounds to lead Germany to victory in the 2009 Meydan Nations Cup
RIGHT: Laura Renwick and Limelight de Breve, whose victory in the 2009 Old Lodge Queen Elizabeth II Cup foiled King's Cup winner Peter Charles of a unique double

016

Twenty20 cricket—and having Nations Cups which dragged on with 20 or so teams taking part was no one's idea of snappy entertainment.

Such Nations Cups continued to take place, of course, but they were minor league affairs, and their main significance was that the top team in this division at the end of the season was promoted to the Super League, and the bottom SSL team was relegated. It gave the necessary 'needle' to the premier series.

BEGINNING OF A NEW ERA

In 2009 it was 'all change' yet again, as Samsung pulled out and the formula was altered, to bring in 10 teams—which seems somewhat perverse, since the number was originally reduced to provide better entertainment—but still to have just eight Nations Cups. A major snag for many of the would-be venues was that although the International Equestrian Federation (FEI) provided, through Dubai-based company Meydan, the 200,000 euro prize-money for the Nations Cup, the shows were individually responsible for finding the same money for the Grand Prix.

After a fair amount of chatter, the same eight shows, including Hickstead, of course, were chosen to stage these premier league Nations Cups. Also significant was the change of the relegation rule, with the two bottom teams dropping out.

Following the British team's run of success at Hickstead up until 1980, the balance became very much less one-sided. In the 29 years since then the home side has won 10 times, France and Germany (West Germany as they were in 1982 and 1984) have seven wins apiece, the United States and Ireland two each and Italy one, in 1994.

That sole Italian success came at what was undoubtedly the nadir of Hickstead's Nations Cup story. Just a few days earlier the final session of the Royal Windsor Horse Show was washed out by torrential rain, and the same furious storm lashed down equally hard in West Sussex. By the final day, Nations Cup day, the International Arena was a sea of mud, and although several of the fences were reduced in size and the time allowed was increased, no one could go clear. Britain ended the first round in the lead, but on a massive score of 24 faults. British team manager Ronnie Massarella, who had asked for course changes that were not made, said: 'The scores speak for themselves. I've said many wonderful things about Hickstead in the past, but this has been a dreadful day.'

In the end the British were beaten by a quarter of a time-fault, but Henk Nooren, Dutch trainer of the Italian team who edged home in front, said that after the first round: 'I did not want to go on. I wanted it to stop.'

It is a measure of the success of the drainage system that has since been installed, and updated at considerable cost to the Bunn exchequer, that when a rainstorm of similar proportion fell in 2007, the surroundings may have deteriorated into a thick brown 'soup', but the arena rode without any real problem.

That year, 1994, was a momentous one as it marked the retirement from Nations Cups of David Broome, who, during a career that lasted for 35 years, rode for the British team no fewer than 108 times, and was on the winning side in 37 of them. No one who saw his magical performances to win the World Championship in La Baule, 1970, will ever forget them, and there were so many more besides. He still makes a huge contribution to British show jumping, especially at his own Wales and the West showground—a Welsh Hickstead?

The French, who were the ones to break the British monopoly in 1981, had not won a Nations Cup in Britain since 1947, the first time it was run after the Second World War. They were led to victory by Patrick Pierre and his exuberant grey Flon Flon who, earlier in the meeting, bridged an even longer gap when becoming the first French winners of a British Grand Prix since 1938.

OPPOSITE PAGE: Shane Breen on Carmena Z, winners of the Queen Elizabeth II Cup in 2008

After landing the World Team Championship in Dublin in 1982 the French returned for another Hickstead success in 1983—the British gained their revenge by winning the French Nations Cup in Paris two weeks later—and then won four times in six years, in 1986, 1988-89 and in 1991.

The line-up for the 1986 Prince of Wales Cup must rank as one of the classiest ever, with the winning side including Pierre Durand on Jappeloup, winners of the Olympic gold medal in Seoul, 1988. The British runners-up included John Whitaker with a Milton at the beginning of his career—team manager Ronnie Massarella said of Milton, with great foresight: 'In another year he will be ready for anything', though, sadly, that 'anything' did not include a trip to Seoul—while in the third-placed German team was Paul Schockemöhle on his mighty Deister.

Paul and Deister, as well as winning two Derbies and one of their three European Championships at Hickstead, had been members of the German teams that won the Prince of Wales Cup in 1982 and 1984, and were in the runners-up squad in 1985 when the British regained the winning thread. Deister and Liz Edgar's Everest Forever jumped the only double clears, but Liz's team-mates, Nick Skelton on Everest Apollo, Grand Prix winners the day before, John Whitaker on Hopscotch and Malcolm Pyrah with Towerlands Anglezarke gave her rather better support.

1986 was also the year when it was announced that professionals would be allowed to ride in the Olympics, giving David Broome the chance for a last hurrah, and so nearly a third medal, in Seoul.

> *'Hickstead has been fantastic for British show jumping, there is nowhere else like it in the country. Douglas had a lot of foresight to give British riders something they would get on the continent and we could not have done what we did without it. There is nothing quite like the Derby anywhere in the world. Just to jump a clear round makes you feel you have achieved something—to win it four times, including on Buddy Bunn for Douglas, was great. And when I was first picked for the British team at Hickstead I thought "Now I've made it!" That was a big stepping stone in my career.'*
>
> JOHN WHITAKER

MILTON'S DOUBLE CLEAR

John Whitaker and Milton showed just what the British Olympic team was to miss when jumping the only double clear in 1988, but that could not keep France out of the winner's enclosure, a situation that was repeated a year later, though in 1989 the United States, including two of the all-female team that triumphed at Hickstead in 1987, squeezed ahead of Britain into second.

Both of the US women riders, Joan Scharffenberger with Victory and Debbie Dolan with VIP, jumped double clears. The stallion VIP left an important legacy at Hickstead, for during his stay there he leaped out of his box and on to one of Sue Bunn's mares, the thoroughbred Sweet Sage, producing the eventing stallion Viceroy, ridden to victory at Blenheim in 2004 by Pippa Funnell.

John Whitaker and Milton jumped a fourth successive double clear for the British team in 1991, but after a jump-off the hosts once again had to give best to France, who then had a lapse until 1998, with Britain winning five of the next six, only sinking in the mud behind Italy in 1994.

Britain used the 1992 Nations Cup to test 'possibles' for the forthcoming Barcelona Olympic Games, and Tina Cassan (now, of course, Mrs Fletcher) staked a big claim

OPPOSITE PAGE: John Whitaker and the mighty Milton, who jumped the only double clear in the 1988 Nations Cup at Hickstead, but was not allowed to travel to Seoul for the Olympic Games

HICKSTEAD

when helping the team on their winning way by jumping a double clear on Fred Brown's Genesis. In the end she did not make it to Spain, named only as reserve, but two of the others in the team, Nick Skelton and Tim Grubb, did so, together with John and Michael Whitaker.

That was an auspicious year for Hickstead: the Royal International Horse Show, the official horse show of The British Horse Society, made its long-awaited return to an outdoor arena, after its sojourn first in the Wembley Arena and then, from 1984, in the National Exhibition Centre, Birmingham. During its time at London's White City the Edward Prince of Wales Cup had been an integral part of the Royal International, but, until 1998, Hickstead ran the Nations Cup at a separate meeting.

So, less than two weeks after playing such a major role in Britain's Nations Cup triumph, Tina and Genesis had one of their own, in the Queen Elizabeth II Cup. It was to be the first of three victories for Tina in what, since its foundation in 1949, had become one of show jumping's most important competitions, if not the most important, for women riders.

Tina and Genesis, who had suffered a slight virus after the Nations Cup meeting, were one of only two combinations to go clear in a five-horse jump-off to foil what would have been the first Australian win in the Queen's Cup, beating Di Dawson and Taxi by more than seven seconds.

Tina retained the Cup in 1993 on Bond Xtra and scored again on Overa in 2007 when the Queen's Cup was run for the last time in its original format. From 2008 women were admitted to the King George V Gold Cup; they had been eligible in 1947 and 1948, but were then excluded after being given, in 1949, the Queen's Cup to compete for. This was now also opened to riders of both sexes, and, appropriately perhaps, the first winner of the 'mixed' Queen Elizabeth II Cup, in 2008, was Douglas Bunn's son-in-law, Shane Breen on Carmena Z, earning him the nickname 'Queen Breen'.

Michael Whitaker's success in the first Hickstead-staged King's Cup, on Midnight Madness, was his third in this historic contest, which dates back to 1911, following Disney Way in 1982 and Didi in 1989, and he was to win again on Midnight Madness in 1994.

The horse had been bought in Canada by Sir Phil (now Lord) Harris for Michael to ride in the Barcelona Olympics: but to be eligible for the Games a horse has to belong to an owner from the same country as the rider on 1st January. Due to an unfortunate technicality, the deal had not been completed in time. He nevertheless proved a more than useful addition to Michael's stable for some years afterwards, while Tim Grubb and Denizen sealed their Barcelona ticket by winning the Grand Prix.

In 1993 the Whitaker brothers, John on Milton and Michael with Midnight Madness,

both with double clears, joined Skelton and David Broome, who had been dropped from the Barcelona team after injuring his back in a fall a week before the Games, to give Britain another Prince of Wales victory.

David Broome, who won the King George V Gold Cup a record six times—the first on Sunsalve in 1960, the last on Lannegan in 1991, the year before it was first staged at Hickstead—said, when he walked the course of the 1993 competition, that he thought the course was the smallest he had ever seen for the King's Cup. But both he on Lannegan and the previous year's winners, Michael Whitaker with Midnight Madness, found it just beyond them.

ONLY SKELTON CLEAR

They were among 11 who shared second place on four faults behind Nick Skelton who, with Limited Edition, had the only first-round clear. It was the first time since the Royal International was restarted in 1947 that the Cup was won in the opening round. These days the rules would not allow that to happen.

This was a second King's Cup victory for Nick, who had already won in 1984 on his great horse St James, and was to enter the winner's enclosure twice more, in 1996 with Cathleen and 1999 on Hopes Are High.

Britain's Olympic horses—including Skelton's mount, Showtime—had already left for Atlanta when Cathleen won, but six weeks earlier Geoff Billington and It's Otto clinched their tickets to the United States with a double clear that led the host team to a wide-margin victory over Ireland and France in the Nations Cup. In Atlanta Billington and It's Otto were in a seven-horse jump-off for the silver and bronze medals, eventually finishing sixth.

Geoff and It's Otto had also helped Britain in the 1995 Prince of Wales Cup in a team that included John Whitaker on Keeley Durham's Welham, which he had only started riding the previous autumn but with which he still produced two clear rounds. The Irish finished last of the six teams, but bounced back the following month when Robert Splaine on Heather Blaze and Marion Hughes with Flo Jo brought off the classic King's and Queen's Cups double.

Splaine and Heather Blaze had dual winners Michael Whitaker and Midnight Madness as their principal victims, while Di Lampard with Abbervail Dream, runners-up to Marion and Flo Jo, were the defending Queen Elizabeth II Cup holders, who went on to regain it in 1998.

Marion had only been allowed to compete at the Royal International after a number of top riders dropped out, and she telephoned to ask if she could enter. Twelve months later she and Flo Jo returned to prove that their first victory was no fluke.

Nick's 1999 victory on Hopes Are High looked improbable a couple of days earlier when, having jumped a first-round clear for Britain in the Nations Cup, the horse then caught a pole between his legs in the practice ring, and was too lame to jump in the second round. With them out of action, the team was narrowly beaten by Germany, who thus had their first Nations Cup win at Hickstead for 15 years.

It was touch-and-go whether Hopes Are High would be able to jump in the King's Cup, but he was sound on the morning of the competition and had the best of a 10-horse jump-off to beat Ludger Beerbaum with Champion du Lys by 0.33sec. This performance

'Hickstead has been part of my life. Those big old trees in the arena were little saplings when I first came here, over 40 years ago. I've been lucky enough to win nearly all the big classes here, grands prix, Nations Cups, the Derby Trial. The only one I did not win was the Derby; I jumped a clear but was in a jump-off with Harvey (Smith) and finished second. It's a spectacle is Hickstead'.

GRAHAM FLETCHER

confirmed his place in the British team for the European Championships—also, of course, at Hickstead, the following month.

When the Royal International and Edward Prince of Wales Nations Cup were finally re-united in 1998, the British team was embroiled in an almost unprecedented run of failure, their worst season since the Nations Cup series had started in 1965. They hoped to rectify the situation at Hickstead but, having won on home ground for the previous three years, now finished only fifth behind the French.

But Robert Smith, who had won the King George V Gold Cup as an 18-year-old in 1979 on Video—which his father Harvey rode to win the British Jumping Derby two years later—and for a second time in 1988 with Boysie, and who was not in the Nations Cup team, restored some pride to the home squad.

He and Mighty Blue had the only clear in the first round of the King's Cup, on ground riding deep after torrential rain, but under the rules of the contest—to make it a better television spectacle—the best four were brought back for a jump-off. Nick Skelton, who had just taken over the ride on Hopes Are High, set a tough target, but justice was done when Smith and Mighty Blue went more than two seconds faster.

Britain went into the 2000 Royal International having broken a Nations Cup famine,

> *'It is a fantastic venue—still the best in our country by a mile. I was very fortunate; when I was 17 I won the Grand Prix of Great Britain at the Nations Cup meeting, so it sort of kick-started me very early. I rode ponies at Hickstead and used to come when there were four shows a year. It has some fantastic events: the Derby, more recently the King's Cup—it is a classic place.'*
>
> ROBERT SMITH

that stretched back for three years without a victory anywhere, in the toughest contest of all, by beating the Germans on home ground in Aachen just two weeks earlier. But they were doomed to more disappointment when the Irish, who were in fantastic form and had already won five Nations Cups that season, made the Prince of Wales Cup their sixth.

No one in the British team was more upset than young Welshman Andrew Davies, who had been devastated when he lost the ride on Hopes Are High to Nick Skelton, but had produced an inspired performance from Captain Wellington in Aachen, to lay down a claim for a place in the Sydney Olympic team.

In Hickstead things could hardly have gone worse for him, as in the first round he was eliminated for starting before the bell: it was a questionable decision by the judges, who had plenty of time to warn him as he circled before he crossed the starting line, and team manager Ronnie Massarella was fuming. But the rule had been broken.

It was still a close-run finish, but a double clear from Dermott Lennon on Liscalgot put Ireland ahead. Their last to go, US-based Kevin Babington with Carling King, could afford only one fence down, and that was all they had, to beat Britain by four faults.

Cameron Hanley completed a great show for the Irish when riding Ballaseyr Twilight to win the King George V Gold Cup, beating 1999 Derby winners Rob Hoekstra and Lionel II. The Isle of Man is not a place usually associated with top-class show jumping, but the Ballaseyr stable, which is based there, brought off a unique double by also taking the Queen Elizabeth II Cup through Claudia Neureiter on Ballaseyr Leonardo. Claudia, the daughter of a lorry driver from Salzburg, who had been living on the Isle of Man for 18 months, was the first Austrian winner of the Queen's Cup.

Ireland's win in 2000 was their first in a British Nations Cup since 1937, but they only had to wait 12 months for their next, which came a month after winning the team gold medal in the European Championships in Arnhem, Holland.

Three of the winning championship team, Peter Charles and Corrada—who a month later began their hat-trick of British Jumping Derby wins—Kevin Babington with Carling King and Dermott Lennon on Liscalgot, were joined by Cian O'Connor on Waterford Crystal (with whom he won, then lost, the Athens Olympic gold medal) at Hickstead, and held off a strong German challenge.

The United States squad came in only fourth, but two of them went on to complete the classic double when Norman dello Joio—competing at Hickstead for the first time for 21 years—on Glasgow, and Candice King with Elu de la Hardière were the only ones to have double clears in the King's and Queen's Cups respectively.

Frank Chapot, the US team trainer, had been the last from his country to win the King George, in 1974. His wife Mary was the only previous US winner of the Queen Elizabeth, back in 1968, but American winners have been in abundance since 2001, with three victories from the final four runnings of the competition before its formula was changed in 2008.

Two of those triumphs, in 2004 and 2006, came from Molly Ashe on Lutopia, with Laura Kraut and Anthem intervening to score in 2005. Molly Ashe had never competed at Hickstead before the first of her two wins, though she had been a regular at many of the top European shows, and had won the Berlin Grand Prix on Kroon Gravin in 2000. With that mare at the end of her career Molly introduced her 'heir-apparent', Lutopia, which she had bought from her ex-husband Eric Hasbrouck three years earlier. Making up for lost time, US riders filled the top three places, with Sheila Burke and Caya beaten by 0.08sec in the jump-off, ahead of Judy Garofalo on Oliver III.

That Lutopia was up to her billing as Kroon Gravin's successor was confirmed when they beat Jane Annett on her course specialist Cullawn Diamond two years later. Dutch rider Angelique Hoorn, third in 2006, had already had her name inscribed on the Queen's Cup roll of honour with Hascal in 2002.

Cameron Hanley, who rode Ballaseyr Twilight to win the King George V Gold Cup in 2000

DOUBLE FOR U.S.

When Laura Kraut and Anthem won the 2005 Queen's Cup they initiated another classic double for their country, with Jeffrey Welles and Armani going on to victory in the King's. Both Kraut and Welles, like Ashe in 2004, were making their Hickstead riding débuts; Jeffrey had been there as a spectator and he was, he said, competing in Europe for the first time for 19 years because he had 'not had a horse good enough' in between. Armani certainly was good enough, and in relegating Nick Skelton and Russel to second place—for the second year in succession—he gave Jeffrey what he described as 'My biggest win ever. A huge honour.' Kraut, who had only ever seen Hickstead on television, had the only clear in the four-horse jump-off on the veteran Anthem to beat compatriot Kimberley Prince with Couletto K James.

Robert Smith celebrates the British team's triumph in the 2006 Nations Cup.

Ireland, having had to wait so long for a British Nations Cup, could easily have made it three in a row in 2002. There has been a great deal of tinkering with Nations Cup rules in recent years, and in 2002 if there was equality of faults after two rounds, each team's collective time in the second was the deciding factor. Germany, led by European Champions Ludger Beerbaum and Gladdys S, finished level with Ireland, for whom Cian O'Connor and Waterford Crystal had the only double clear of the entire competition, but the Germans were just over a second faster.

Ludger, then the World No 1 rider, swapped to the dimutive but talented Champion du Lys to gain his first success in the King George V Gold Cup. With a brilliant jump-off round he foiled the young British rider Richard Davenport, at that time based in Holland with Jan Tops, on Enjoleuse de l'Eaugrenee, who had the only other jump-off clear.

If British riders were being individually frustrated in the King's and Queen's Cups, their Nations Cup team did get back on course in 2003, thanks mainly to Nick Skelton and Arko III, the horse that had inspired his return to competitive riding after he broke his neck in a fall in 2000. Nick was in the wars again at that Hickstead meeting and had to take a massive dose of pain-killers after ricking his back on the morning of the Nations Cup, but neither that nor the rain-soaked ground could prevent him giving Arko every assistance as they cleared each fence twice.

With Richard Davenport again proving his ability, on Luc, and Robert Smith also clear with Mr Springfield, Scott Smith's four faults on Cabri d'Elle could be discarded, and second time round Robert was not needed, as the others had ensured a British success. Ireland and France were equal second.

Although Kevin Babington, by now a regular commuter from his home in Pennsylvania to the top European shows, and Carling King could not quite help Ireland to another

team success, their two clear rounds in the King George V Gold Cup were all that was needed to add this to the British Grand Prix they had won at Hickstead two years earlier. William Funnell on Comex, just back from winning the Swedish Derby, and Andrew Davies on Limbo V filled the minor placings.

The records say that Helena Weinberg on Albführens Ramonus was the first German winner of the Queen Elizabeth II Cup since Anna Clement in 1959, but Helena was born in Britain and had considerable international success as Miss Dickinson (her brother Bruce was the lead singer with Iron Maiden) before marrying fellow rider Peter Weinberg and going to live in Germany.

Robert Smith with Mr Springfield and Richard Davenport on Luc were back again in Britain's successful team in 2004, but Nick Skelton had to change to Russel, as Arko III—who was being aimed as one of Britain's two individuals qualified for the Athens Olympics, together with Robert and Mr Springfield—had mucus in his throat and lungs. Robert Whitaker on Qualite came in to join the team, who looked to have blown their chances when after the first round they were only among four teams sharing third place behind Ireland and Holland.

Smith and Mr Springfield were clear twice, and Richard with Luc was also faultless second time round. But Robert Whitaker retired Qualite after hitting four, so it all depended on Skelton. He could not afford a fence down, and he had fallen off when Russel put in a sudden stop in the first round. Now he returned for a determined single time-fault in the second, and the team beat the French by three faults.

Nick and Russel won the next day's Grand Prix, but in the King George V Gold Cup they had to give way to Germany's Rene Tebbel on Farina, a daughter of the great stallion For Pleasure, winner of two Olympic team golds. Tebbel said after his win: 'I have been coming to Hickstead for seven or eight years and winning nothing.' He was in the winner's enclosure again in 2005, with his three team mates, after the Edward Prince of Wales Cup. With the US team right on their tails, Tebbel came in last for Germany, this time on Quel Homme, without a fence to spare, and able to have just one time-fault if they were to win. That is precisely what he had.

BRITAIN'S GRANDSTAND FINISH

The home side, trying for a third successive home win, flopped into fifth place, but regained the winning thread in 2006 with a grandstand finish to overtake the French. France led at halfway, after only William Funnell and his subsequent triple Derby winner Cortaflex Mondriaan could go clear for Britain. Second time around, first Robert Smith with Marius Claudius, with a clear, and then Michael Whitaker on Mozart des Hayettes,

'What Douglas Bunn achieved at Hickstead is comparable only to what has been built up at Aachen using the talents of the entire German Federation. Without his foresight, British show jumping would be lacking an arena of international importance. I hope the young up-and-coming riders appreciate this tremendous contribution to our sport. His energy and enthusiasm created a fabulous venue to showcase the sport and to provide our riders and horses with invaluable experience of top-level competition in a truly international-standard arena. We must remember that Hickstead is also a venue for international dressage competition at the very highest level. The whole Bunn family have supported Douglas throughout the years and we wish them every success in continuing to build on his legacy to carry Hickstead to even greater heights.'

DI LAMPARD

GENERALI
GENERALI

with one time-fault, put Britain back in contention; the team needed a final clear from John Whitaker on Peppermill. He had only started riding the nine-year-old that February, but John had already won the San Patrignano Grand Prix on him, and now he showed that precision at measuring his fences which has so often underpinned his consistent success.

The meeting was a test of 'possibles' for the forthcoming World Championships in Aachen, and Skelton's Arko III, who had had a disappointing season, was totally ruled out when he fell heavily in the King's Cup. It was the sort of fall that had broken Nick's neck six years earlier, but at least this time, thankfully, he could walk away. Heinrich Engemann and Aboyeur, for Germany, had one of only two first-round clears, but Roger-Yves Bost with Idéal de la Loge easily had their measure when it came to a timed barrage.

This was the first French victory in the King George V Gold Cup since their great champion, Pierre Jonquères d'Oriola, won on Marquis III in 1947—when the show was restarted after the Second World War. As is so often the case, though there is no logical reason why, it was quickly followed up by another. Twelve months later Aymeric de Ponnat with Jubilee d'Ouilly led home a Gallic one-two-three, ahead of Jerome Debas Montagner on Idem de B'Neville and Christian Harmon on Ephebe For Ever.

De Ponnat, making his Hickstead début, had ridden since he was very young but only began competing internationally in 2007 and was ranked a mere 143rd among the world's riders. He had broken-in Jubilee as a three-year-old and brought her up steadily over the next seven years. Winning that season's Eindhoven Grand Prix earned him selection for Hickstead, which was, he said: 'Like a fairytale. The organisation, the quality of the courses, the timing, everything, is truly great.' Sadly his fairytale did not have a happy ending, as he lost the ride on Jubilee, and other horses in the same ownership, later that season.

Also in 2007, Molly Cawley (formerly Ashe), who was three-and-a-half months pregnant, and Lutopia, trying for a third success in what was to be the last-ever 'women only' Queen Elizabeth II Cup, had to settle for second place behind Tina Fletcher and Overa. Before that they had helped their side to a narrow victory over Britain in the Nations Cup.

At this, the 100th anniversary of Britain's oldest international show, the British were firm favourites and looked as if they would justify that position when leading after the first round. A determined clear from Michael Whitaker on Suncal Portofino, a time-fault for William Funnell's Cortaflex Mondriaan and one down by Nick Skelton on Russel, left them seven faults clear of the joint seconds, an all-women US team, and Holland.

The Americans went in to the contest lying bottom of the Samsung Super League and in desperate need of points to avoid relegation. When the British, for whom only Nick Skelton and Russel could manage a second-round clear, gave them half a chance, they seized it avidly. Molly, now on Cocu, Laura Kraut with her 2005 Queen's Cup winner Anthem, and Beezie Madden with Judgement all went clear and pipped Britain at the post.

The 2008 Royal International was run in the shadow of the up-coming Olympic Games, with the equestrian competitions in Hong Kong, as a result of which many of the top international horses were missing. Germany had the best of a high-scoring Edward Prince of Wales Cup after Britain had squandered their first-round lead, but if nothing else, it proved that, in Charlotte Platt, the home side has a rider with a big future. The 22-year-old, who won a team gold in the 2007 European Young Riders' Championships, had asked if she could be in the Super League team at Hickstead, which is only two miles from her home. Her wish was granted, and with a double clear on Paulien II—the only one in the competition—her self-confidence was totally justified.

Michael Whitaker and Wonami van den Aard, making her Super League début, were also clear first time, and a repetition of that in the second round would have forced a jump-off with the improving Germans. But one mistake dropped the British to equal second with Sweden, both on 28 faults to Germany's 24.

OPPOSITE PAGE: The French team parading before the Meydan FEI Nations Cup in 2009. Roger-Yves Bost, winner of the King George V Gold Cup in 2006; Kevin Staut, European Champion in 2009; Olivier Guillon.

WULSCHNER'S KING GEORGE

Holger Wulschner and Clausen, who clinched the German victory, jumped two more clear rounds to take the King George V Gold Cup. Clausen was injured while travelling to Spain in the spring, which cost them any chance of Olympic selection, but Wulschner won the Grand Prix in Norten-Hardenberg on him before going on to Hickstead. He said that there had been so many offers for the horse that, two weeks before their King's Cup victory, the owner, Siegfried Kludt, had sold Wulschner a half-share for one Euro, and given the other half to his two-year-old daughter to remove any temptation to sell.

Women were able to ride in the King's Cup for the first time since 1948, but the best-placed of them was US rider Nicole Shahinian-Simpson, who finished fifth on Dragonfly. And as already noted, Shane Breen took advantage of the change of rules to win the Queen Elizabeth II Cup, on Carmena Z.

Defending his title, Shane, again on Carmena Z, was among a sextet of men who jumped off for the 2009 Queen's Cup, sponsored by Old Lodge, but all were put in their place by the only woman to reach the barrage, Laura Renwick, and her superbly-consistent mare Limelight de Brève. Laura has brought 'Lulu', as she is known, up through the novice ranks to international status, and now they had just too much pace for Peter Charles with Olga White's Murkas Rupert R.

They thus foiled what would have been an historic double, as, the following day, Peter rode Sandra Cordiner's Murkas Pall Mall H to victory in the Longines King George V Gold Cup. In this the first British success in the King's Cup since Nick Skelton won on Hopes Are High ten years earlier, Peter led a one-two-three for the home side, ahead of Tim Stockdale on John Bosher's Fresh Direct Corlato and Ben Maher with Robin Hood W.

Peter and Pall Mall were first to go in a seven-horse jump-off, and the only ones clear a second time, to land Britain's biggest show jumping prize, worth £50,000 to the winner. Peter said afterwards that he felt his time was beatable but that he wanted to be sure of going clear: 'It's like a game of chess, going first. But I've been trying to win the King's Cup for more than 20 years.'

Both second and third were indeed faster, but at a cost. Ben Maher and Robin Hood lost their chance of success when lowering the first fence: they then chased hard for a share of the lucrative place-money, but were deprived of second by Tim and Corlato, who were .05sec faster and would have won but for clouting the final fence.

Corlato had only just returned from a long break, first to have embryo transplants and then suffering from anaemia and a virus, so Tim said beforehand that he thought she might tire towards the end of the competition. But, urged on by the spectators who had taken the gallant grey mare to their hearts, she showed all her old enthusiasm and only just failed.

It was a much happier competition for the British riders than the Edward Prince of Wales Cup, the penultimate in the new Meydan FEI Nations Cup series, had been. After torrential rain the arena surface was not at its best, but there were enough clear rounds for this not to be a valid excuse by the home side.

Ben Maher and Robin Hood got home for just four faults in the first round—before collecting nine in the second—but both Robert Smith on Raging Bull Vangelis S (who had only a time-fault in the King's Cup), and Tim Gredley's Omelli, finished the round on 12 faults apiece. These had to count when Peter Charles's Murkas Pom d'Ami knocked up 24. In the second round, Pom d'Ami was better, on nine faults; Vangelis one fault worse, on 13, while Omelli was found to have a slight leg problem which prevented him jumping again.

They finished seventh of the eight teams, yet two weeks later Charles, Stockdale and Maher, on the same horses as in the Prince of Wales Cup, together with Geoff Billington on Rosinus, were joint runners-up in Dublin.

At Hickstead, France increased their lead over the United States at the top of the

table—and eventually won the league—even though, after a jump-off, they had to give best to the German team, who repeated their 2008 success. Penelope Leprevost led the way for France with a clear on the 2007 King's Cup winner (when ridden by Aymeric de Ponnat) Jubilee d'Ouilly, well supported by 2006 King's Cup winner Roger-Yves Bost with Idéal de la Loge and Kevin Staut on Kraque Boom, on four faults apiece.

But the undoubted stars of the competition were Germany's Janne Friederike Meyer and her 11-year-old Cellagon Lambrasco, who had the only double clear in the initial two rounds. With Max Kühner on Acantus and Andreas Knippling, the only one who had been in the winning 2008 team, on Neolisto van het Mierenhof, getting round for one mistake each, Germany matched France's first-round eight-fault total, and again their 16 in the second.

They finished on 24-fault totals, well ahead of third-placed Ireland, on 40, with Sweden pulling themselves clear of relegation by taking fourth place, and Belgium and the United States sharing fifth in front of Britain and Holland. Italy, languishing at the bottom of the league, and Switzerland did not make the second round.

The principals had to jump-off for pride of place. French chef d'équipe Laurent Elias chose their most experienced combination, Roger-Yves with Idéal de la Loge, to represent them, but when they clipped the top plank at the fifth of the seven fences, the door was left open for their rivals.

'Hickstead is my favourite show in the whole world. The atmosphere in the ring is fantastic. I've won three Queen's Cups at Hickstead, jumped in a winning Nations Cup, been second in the Derby. I've had a lot of success here and I love it. And it has made British show jumping—it is the place to go.'

TINA FLETCHER

Janne Friederike, who comes from Hamburg—'That's why I am used to riding in the rain'—was the German choice, and said afterwards that she felt no pressure. The 28-year-old had been riding Cellagon Lambrasco for four years, and said 'He's small, but you would not think so in the ring—he always wants to jump clear. You can never be sure, but I had a good feeling.'

Her confidence was justified, with a third magnificent clear, and her good feeling was echoed by Germany's chef d'équipe Sönke Sönksen, a long-time supporter of Hickstead, who said: 'These riders have fulfilled a wonderful dream for me. I'm sure my friend Douglas was looking down on us with a smile.'

Both Graham and Tina Fletcher have found Hickstead to be a very happy hunting ground.

Nations Cups – Winners Since 1947

(Held at Hickstead in 1971 and from 1975 until the present, except for 1997)

1947	France
1948	USA
1949	Great Britain
1950	Great Britain
1951	Great Britain
1952	Great Britain
1953	Great Britain
1954	Great Britain
1955	Italy
1956	Great Britain
1957	Great Britain
1958	USA
1959	USA
1960	USA
1961	Italy
1962	West Germany
1963	Great Britain
1964	Great Britain
1965	Italy
1966	Not held
1967	Great Britain
1968	USA
1969	West Germany
1970	Great Britain
1971	Great Britain
1972	Great Britain
1973	West Germany
1974	Great Britain
1975	Great Britain
1976	West Germany
1977	Great Britain
1978	Great Britain
1979	Great Britain
1980	Great Britain
1981	France
1982	West Germany
1983	France
1984	West Germany
1985	Great Britain
1986	France
1987	USA
1988	France
1989	France
1990	Great Britain
1991	France
1992	Great Britain
1993	Great Britain
1994	Italy
1995	Great Britain
1996	Great Britain
1997	Great Britain
1998	France
1999	Germany
2000	Ireland
2001	Ireland
2002	Germany
2003	Great Britain
2004	Great Britain
2005	Germany
2006	Great Britain
2007	USA
2008	Germany
2009	Germany

Cian O'Connor and Kevin Babington celebrate Ireland's Nations Cup victory in 2000

King George V Gold Cup – Winners At Hickstead

1992 Michael Whitaker on Everest Midnight Madness (GB)
1993 Nick Skelton on Everest Limited Edition (GB)
1994 Michael Whitaker on Everest Midnight Madness (GB)
1995 Robert Splaine on Heather Blaze (Ireland)
1996 Nick Skelton on Cathleen (GB)
1997 John Whitaker on Virtual Village Welham (GB)
1998 Robert Smith on Senator Mighty Blue (GB)
1999 Nick Skelton on Hopes Are High (GB)
2000 Cameron Hanley on Ballaseyr Twilight (Ireland)
2001 Norman dello Joio on Glasgow (USA)
2002 Ludger Beerbaum on Champion du Lys (Germany)
2003 Kevin Babington on Carling King (Ireland)
2004 Rene Tebbel on Farina (Germany)
2005 Jeffery Welles on Armani (USA)
2006 Roger-Yves Bost on Idéal de la Loge (France)
2007 Aymeric de Ponnat on Jubilee d'Ouilly (France)
2008 Holger Wulschner on Clausen (Germany)
2009 Peter Charles on Murkas Pall Mall H (GB)

Queen Elizabeth II Cup – Winners At Hickstead

1992 Tina Cassan on Genesis (GB)
1993 Tina Cassan on Bond Xtra (GB)
1994 Di Lampard on Abbervail Dream (GB)
1995 Marion Hughes on Flo Jo (Ireland)
1996 Marion Hughes on Flo Jo (Ireland)
1997 Lynne Bevan on Grafton Magna (GB)
1998 Di Lampard on Abbervail Dream (GB)
1999 Jessica Kürten on Paavo N (Ireland)
2000 Claudia Neureiter on Ballaseyr Leonardo (Austria)
2001 Candice King on Elu de la Hardiere (USA)
2002 Angelique Hoorn on Hascal (Holland)
2003 Helena Weinberg on Albführens Ramonus (Germany)
2004 Molly Ashe on Lutopia (USA)
2005 Laura Kraut on Anthem (USA)
2006 Molly Ashe on Lutopia (USA)
2007 Tina Fletcher (Cassan) on Overa (GB)
2008 Shane Breen on Carmena Z (Ireland)
2009 Laura Renwick on Limelight de Breve (GB)

Aymeric de Ponnat, who won the centennial running of the King George V Gold Cup in 2005

37
191

Showing at Hickstead

by Margaret Shaw

'For five days, all roads lead to the All England Jumping Course, where owners, riders and their connections set up camp and enjoy the sport, camaraderie and hospitality that are the trademark qualities of this great show.'

The Royal International Horse Show, the official show of the British Horse Society, has had a few homes in its illustrious 101-year history, but since 1992 it has settled comfortably in West Sussex, where towards the end of July the Bunn family annually hosts the biggest party of the showing season.

The first Longines Royal International Horse Show following Douglas Bunn's death was never going to be an easy one. The show came during a deep recession, with the so-called 'credit crunch' blamed for poor entries at many fixtures. However, despite all the gloom, the 2009 show continued to act as a magnet, and the crème de la crème of the showing world descended on Hickstead.

For five days, all roads led to the All England Jumping Course, where owners, riders and their connections set up camp and enjoyed the sport, camaraderie and hospitality that are the trademark qualities of this great show.

Roger Stack, who has been the Royal International's showing director since 2001, was always upbeat, and was proved right when the entries poured in, to produce the usual bumper show. A former dealer, producer, rider and judge, Roger is celebrating his 60th year in showing, and brings a wealth of experience to his post.

Roger and his wife Bridget have been friends of the Bunn family for more than 40 years, and it was a chance conversation over the dinner table that proved the catalyst for introducing showing rings at Hickstead. While Douglas Bunn always nurtured an ambition to develop an international show-jumping arena, his wife Sue was interested in showing.

Roger remembers: 'Douglas had been to Newmarket and bought a lot of yearlings, because they were cheap, brought them home to Hickstead, and tipped them out in the field. Sue persuaded him to let me break them in, and she started with the two she liked best. They were a lovely grey, Open Mind, and Welsh Version, who was also nice but not as good. I had a lad working for me and the first time he sat on Open Mind he cantered round and shouted "Wembley, here we come!", and he was right. It would be fair to say that if it had not been for Sue's interest in showing, and the success she had with Open Mind and Welsh Version, there would have been no Ring 5, and no showing at Hickstead, at least until the Royal International came. Before that it was entirely due to Sue Bunn.'

Roger, who is extremely proud to carry on the legacy, discipline and high principles of his predecessor, the late Dick Saunders, has seen a lot of changes over the years, many of which have helped raise the popularity of showing. 'In my early days, travelling horses any distance was a long-winded affair. Pre-motorway, travelling from Essex to Surrey involved an overnight journey of four hours to avoid the traffic because you had to go through the centre of London. I was probably one of the last people to take a horse off a train at King's Cross Station, but the present road system and size and speed of the modern horsebox make life much easier for exhibitors,' says Roger.

'The norm when Hickstead started its showing classes was to drive a 20ft four-horse Bedford TK—two facing forward and two facing back—with side and rear ramps. Roy Trigg had one of the first and there was great excitement when it arrived. In those days, grooms and riders 'roughed it' in the back, with a tatty old piece

CENTRE: Roger Stack, Hickstead's showing director since 2001
PAGE 130: Starting young: a leading-rein class being judged on the River Lawn at the Royal International Horse Show.

TOP (LEFT TO RIGHT): Sue Bunn and Open Mind after winning the Supreme Hunter Championships at Hickstead in 1975; ***Guy Landau, stepson of legendary showman, Roy Trigg, with John Dunlop's Supreme Hunter champion, Finn McCool III; Christine Dick being congratulated by Sam Marsh after winning the British Driving Derby at Hickstead in 1968 with Commodore, the first of her 11 successes.***

BOTTOM (LEFT TO RIGHT): Hickstead Patron, Georgina Andrews, with her outstanding side saddle winner, Overdrive II; Douglas Bunn's oldest daughter, Claudia, with her stunning grey, Elektra, at

TOP (LEFT TO RIGHT): TV presenter David Coleman, Daisy Bunn's godfather and a Hickstead director (left) and former Horse & Hound *Editor, Michael Clayton (right) present Dick Saunders, a Grand National winning jockey and Showing Director of the RIHS for over 10 years, with the Dorian Williams Trophy; Robert Walker and Magnus Nicholson sitting it out*

BOTTOM (LEFT TO RIGHT): The Hon. Mrs Janet Kidd with her Fjord ponies Maple Brantly and Maple Augusta, winners of the British Driving Derby at Hickstead in 1974 and 1977; Lady Kirkham's Small Hunter champion, Sporting Sam, ridden by Simon Reynolds; Working Hunter Pony champion, Peeping Tom II, ridden by Thomas Janis

of carpet and Z beds,' recalls Roger. Feeding arrangements for humans could leave something to be desired too: mostly self-catering with, if you were lucky, a two-ring gas stove to cook the bacon for your sandwiches.

'Those were the good old days,' maintains Roger, who can only stand and watch in amazement as the modern 10-horse wagon, with living space and every modern convenience, sweeps through the gate.

Roger considers himself lucky to have seen the end of one showing era, where he competed alongside the likes of Roy Trigg, Vin Toulson and John Rawding, and the beginning of another, as permanent showgrounds, and Hickstead in particular, continue to expand, modernise and make life more bearable for competitors.

The Dick Saunders Pavilion and the Roy Trigg Stand at ring three are just a couple of Roger's innovations, and there are more to come. 'We run shows for the exhibitors' benefit, not the other way round. We listen to what people want, and the pavilion and stand are great focal points for showing enthusiasts. We used to be considered the poor relations, but not any more—this sport is on the up and up,' says Roger.

Over the years, the number of showing classes on the schedule has increased considerably. The Royal International programme now includes a solid nine hours of coloured classes—skewbald and piebald—for horses and ponies. Slots have been found for Mountain and Moorlands; the popular Retraining of Racehorses Championship; and miniature horses, which attract a worldwide following.

The schedule continues to expand. The maxi cob division—new for 2009 and introduced for exhibitors whose true cobs have grown over the 15.1hh mark—generated great interest and was won by Kim Chapman's Dylan Thomas. 'We have to move with the times and give exhibitors what they need,' says Roger.

Amateur classes, too, are an integral part of the Royal International.

'In my opinion, amateur riders are the backbone of our sport. Gone are the days when the professionals had all the best horses and amateurs rode their "pets",' maintains Roger. 'Although professionals set the standards and remain helpful to up-and-coming riders, the gap is narrowing. Nowadays, amateur riders have good horses, their presentation is excellent and their ringcraft's superb. At Hickstead, we encourage them big time.'

One such exhibitor is Cheshire-based Irene Susca, who realised a lifelong ambition when winning the amateur hunter title with Swansea Gale at the 2008 Royal International. A finalist since 1992, Irene travels the length and breadth of the country to gain her ticket to Hickstead. 'It gets harder and harder to qualify, and we'd been knocking on the door for a long time, so winning that sash meant the world to me,' she remembers. 'It's pure enjoyment for me at Hickstead. With the hard work done in qualifying, we come to enjoy the week, and at the end of it I still love my horse whatever the result.' Irene says the luxury of competing in individual weight classes at the Royal International is sheer bliss. 'Normally, amateurs just have an open class or lightweight and heavyweight divisions, so including middleweights here is a great idea.'

Rider and producer Robert Walker, who has claimed the Supreme Ridden Horse title twice in the past four years, looks on Hickstead as a mid-season holiday. He invariably qualifies a full complement of riding horses, hunters, hacks, cobs and coloureds, and says the show gives him a wonderful opportunity to socialise with his owners. 'We map out the Royal International qualifiers, so during the early part of the season we seem to be constantly on the road, but here we set up camp and stay for the week. Mostly we compete in one section a day, so that gives us ample time to sit down and relax,' he says. 'The Royal International has a great atmosphere, my owners love it, and they all watch and support each other's horses.'

Having been a Hickstead finalist since 1992, Robert is the first to admit that Royal

International championships are not the easiest in which to ride. 'With the sheer numbers forward, there's definitely an art to showing here. You may only get two passes in front of the judges, so you have to be spot on,' he says.

Most exhibitors staying for the week favour a change-round of horses at the halfway stage, relying on grooms or professional transporters to drive a second lorry to Hickstead. For pony producer Julie Templeton, the Royal International invariably presents a logistical nightmare, as she brings up to 28 ponies and 24 riders—aged from three to 25—to compete. But, having already done the rounds and managed to get each pony and rider to the right show to collect their qualifying ticket, Julie copes with consummate ease at Hickstead. 'A party atmosphere prevails all week. It's one of the season's highlights and it means the world to the kids to qualify.' she says.

Jeff Osborne, one of Hickstead's greatest supporters, at full speed in the Osborne Refrigerators Double Harness Scurry Championship

Debbie Thomas is another producer who burns plenty of midnight oil to qualify her charges. Based slightly off the beaten track in South Wales, Debbie recalls one weekend that saw her show team travel first to Lancashire, returning to their Camarthen yard at 12.30am. The home-based team had already loaded a second lorry with ponies, which meant Debbie was pulling out of the yard again at 1am to drive to Kent County. 'We made our classes by the skin of our teeth,' says Debbie, who went through the same operation to take a third team to Stithians in Cornwall. 'It's fortunate we've got good people at home and a rota of drivers,' she adds.

A multitude of home-produced ponies also grace Hickstead's showing rings and the BSPS Pretty Polly classes—open to those who choose to produce ponies without professional help—have proved extremely popular.

In recent years, two of the youngest jockeys have carried off the overall championship. Abbie Dymond and Okewood Delightful were victorious in 2007, while Jess Renshaw-Smith savoured every moment of her 2008 lap of honour in the International Arena on Nantcol Lady Penelope, as did sister Georgia 12 months later in her first season with Kingsford Sweet Story.

No Royal International story would be complete without mentioning the working hunter course, which is purpose-built, using the natural obstacles for which the venue is so famous, though they caused quite a furore when first introduced. Clear rounds are always at a premium over Kevin Millman's track and there is no doubt that Hickstead's working hunter specialists are husband-and-wife team Robert and Louise Bell. From 1995, riding nine different horses, they have recorded no fewer than 14 wins and 10 championships between them, and on three occasions have filled both champion and reserve slots, all

on horses that hunt regularly throughout the season. 'The course was designed for true working hunters, and any horse that follows hounds should jump round without any problem. It's the best class to win by a country mile,' says Robert. This sentiment is echoed by Louise: 'A win here means more than any other.'

Jayne Webber, who was supreme champion and reserve in 2008 with The Philanderer and Red Andes, and took the 2009 coloured horse champion and reserve with The Humdinger and Red Andes, believes the Royal International is the one true outdoor championship show. 'The supreme title had always eluded me, so to win in the international arena with all my friends and family present meant more than anything,' she said.

The 2009 supreme champion Guy Landau was another rider very keen to add the Royal International accolade to his enviable list of achievements with champion hunter Finn McCool, owned by racehorse trainer John Dunlop, who won the supreme in 1997 and 1998 with Red Hand. 'This is the one everyone wants to win. I'm very proud to have clinched it this year,' Guy said.

Roger Stack and the team at Hickstead can feel justifiably proud that showing connections hold the Royal International in such high esteem.

'It's a great team effort. We have in place wonderful sponsors, superb stewards and I take my hat off to Edward and Lizzie Bunn and their hard-working ground and office staff,' says Roger. Far from resting on their laurels, the team at Hickstead uphold Douglas Bunn's legacy, and subtle changes continue to be made. In 2009 in the working hunter ring, the stone wall was modified to include 'knock down' bricks, and a cut-and-laid hedge was used for the first time in many years. Themed fences continue to appear, and, also in 2009, a Norfolk dyke made its début. 'And we're not finished yet,' added Roger Stack, whose presence around the rings seems assured for quite some time. He said: 'I've been told showing directors don't retire, they just keep going till they drop—what a way to go!'

Across the Country

'Three of them galloped straight into the ditch and turned over. There were bodies, loose horses everywhere– it was chaos. But we used to have such fun.' – SUE BUNN

In 1974 Douglas decided that even the huge International Arena was not big enough to fulfil all his plans. Always a keen hunting man, and for some years joint-master of the Mid-Surrey Farmers' Draghounds, he dreamed up a cross-country competition that was to prove immensely popular and now, as Team Chasing, is spread throughout the British Isles.

It was intended as just 'a bit of fun', but it was taken very seriously, or at least very competitively, by those who took part. Teams of five (there are only four in Team Chasing squads these days) would set off, usually in a headlong gallop, over or through whatever fences were set before them, and the time of the last of the best four would count.

There could hardly have been a more distinguished quintet than that which won the inaugural competition: although officially the 'Dressage Team'—this was way before Team Chasers thought up all sorts of outlandish names for themselves—they were actually eventers, and included Mary Gordon-Watson on Cornishman V, the only combination ever to hold World, European and Olympic titles at the same time, together with Suzanne Lumb, Anna Collins, Marjorie Comerford and Carol Newton.

Mary, now Mrs Low, recalls: 'There was already an eventing team, so we were asked to be the dressage team. We took some persuading to do it, it was such a new thing, but we had such fun. We rode across country in our top hats, and I did a lot of team chasing afterwards, though not much at Hickstead.'

She and 'Corny' did compete again the second year though, when it nearly ended in disaster for them, as it did for Marjorie Comerford's young event horse Fly Lane, who fell and broke his neck at the second fence. Cornishman, who treated with disdain the obstacles at Punchestown, Haras du Pin, Mexico (with Richard Meade) and Munich, slipped taking off at a post-and-rail, landed on it, and straddled the fence for minutes before he could be manoeuvred off.

Mary said: 'I think that was the biggest team chase course I ever went over. It was quite scary going over those big timber fences on a horse who was racing, which he was, with the other horses around him, because he had been point-to-pointed by my father. He only had three races but it made him very hot with other horses, so he was very, very strong.'

Mary took Cornishman in more conventional competitions at Hickstead, too, winning a Grade C Championship there, and a Parcours de Chasse for eventers: 'It was a bit like the Eventers Grand Prix they have now. We jumped the Devil's Dyke and the Bank, through the water, all the exciting things, and he was very careful that day. We did have a fence down going into the Dyke, but I think almost everybody did, and we went very fast.

'It was actually one of the most exciting things that ever happened to me, because I was not very good at show jumping. So I enjoyed that more than almost any other competition.'

At the 1975 Easter meeting, the second running of the team cross-country was the only competition that survived. There had been several inches of snow the night before, and everything else had to be cancelled. But the show jumpers still had their way, and won what developed into a battle of attrition.

Lionel Dunning, who had never ridden in a cross-country competition before, led the way for them, with Ted Edgar, the late Ray Howe, Stephen Hadley and Bob Ellis—now, of course, the main-ring course designer at Hickstead—in hectic support.

Sue Bunn, who with Douglas rode for the Mid-Surrey Farmers Drag team, remembers it well: 'The show jumpers were determined to win, and they came roaring down to the last, which was a hedge with a ditch towards them. Three of them galloped straight into the ditch and turned over. There were bodies, loose horses everywhere—it was chaos. But we used to have such fun.'

Edgar, Howe and Hadley were the three who came to grief at the last. They remounted and finished, and then two of them (though no one can remember which two!) had to go to hospital to be checked over.

PAGE 138: Eddie Macken, four times a Derby winner, leads his team-mates over the Bank

ABOVE: Lucinda Fredericks with Badminton, Burghley and Lexington winner, Headley Britannia, who triumphed in the Hickstead Eventing Grand Prix in 2004
TOP RIGHT: Mary Gordon-Watson and her Olympic eventing gold medallist Cornishman V, after winning the Eventing Parcours de Chasse
BOTTOM RIGHT: Bob Ellis, before his course building days, a member of the Show Jumping Team that won the 1975 Team Cross-Country

Pippa Funnell and The Tourmaline Rose, winners of the inaugural Eventing Grand Prix in 1998, and again in 2000 and 2001

Sue rode in the team cross-country for three years: 'I was always lead-horse for the Mid-Surrey Drag. I used to whip in for them, but the huntsman's horse used to get a bit worried in front, and he'd say to me "You lead off", so I used to virtually hunt the hounds. Fortunately Duggie was there behind me. So when it came to the team chase they'd say "Well, you've got to go in front, Sue. You always do".'

They finished third in 1975, with Malcolm Wallace and Bill Thatcher (who the previous week had both ridden in the Royal Artillery Gold Cup at Sandown Park) in the King's Troop RHA team which finished runners-up.

Sadly, the spring show, and with it the team cross-country, came to an end after a few years. Sue Bunn explained: 'It was always at Easter, and when Easter was early the weather was usually awful. Like in 1975. And if you had a really wet Easter show it finished the ground for the whole year, so finally Douglas decided we couldn't have a spring show any more. And by June or July people had turned their horses out, so we couldn't have the cross-country then. But team chasing has gone on from strength to strength.'

Some 20 years later, in 1998, the Eventing Grand Prix was started: a joint project between Douglas Bunn, Paul Schockemöhle and former top international three-day eventer Robert Lemieux. Paul had told Douglas that he thought eventing in Germany was under threat and that a shortened hybrid version, containing show jumps and cross-

'Douglas Bunn was an outstanding businessman, able to hold his ground even in the most difficult situations. His friendly manner, fine sense of humour and generosity made a deep impression on all those who were fortunate enough to have met him.'

FRANK KEMPERMANN (CHIO Aachen)

country fences, which could also be knocked down—at the cost of time penalties—might be the future of the sport. Robert was asked to design the course and from the start found the right degree of difficulty. That it was indeed what the public wanted was proved when more than 18,000, the biggest ever midweek crowd at Hickstead, came to see it.

Unlike the team cross-country this was an individual competition, starting and finishing in the International Arena, but in between galloping up through Douglas's 'front garden'. It was billed as a confrontation between show jumpers and event riders, and the latter have had the best of it so far, especially Pippa Funnell, who rode Anne Burnett's The Tourmaline Rose to victory in the first, and again in 2000 and 2001. Gary Parsonage joined her as the winning-most rider in 2009.

That first Eventing Grand Prix was a particular challenge for the show jumpers, as it started with a dressage test (dropped after a couple of years) which was won by that year's Badminton winners, Chris Bartle and Word Perfect II. But Pippa and The Tourmaline Rose had the only faultless cross-country round, with the late Polly Phillipps on her Bramham winner Coral Cove second and Atlanta Olympic gold medallists Blyth Tait and Ready Teddy third.

Among the most distinguished winners is Lucinda Fredericks's Headley Britannia, who triumphed in 2004 and has gone on since to win the three major three-day events, Burghley, Badminton and Lexington, Kentucky.

Michael Whitaker was the first show jumper to win, in 2003, but he was on an event horse, Chris Ward's Sir Dino. Not until 2006 did a show-jumping horse, Regina Hammell's Mullaghdrin Gold Rain, ridden by Hickstead-based Shane Breen, come home in front despite nearly falling in the water. Shane reckoned that it was his considerable experience in the hunting field that saved the day. Shane, who with his wife Chloe, Douglas Bunn's daughter, runs a thriving equestrian business at Hickstead, tried again, with Dorada, in 2009, when it was sponsored by Quantum Saddles. He beat off a strong challenge from his younger brother Trevor (who helps run the Irish side of their Breen Equestrian business) on Adventure de Kannan, only to be pipped by the last-to-go holders of the title, Gary Parsonage with Peter Street.

Gary, who has ridden in three-day events for Britain at Olympic, World and European Championship level, also won the second Eventing Grand Prix in 1999 on Just So, and thus equalled Pippa Funnell as the most successful rider in the competition. He won the two-star international event at Burgie on Peter Street in 2003, but said after his 2009 win that he keeps Peter Street almost exclusively for show jumping now. Since their 2008 success the horse had had just one cross-country school to get him tuned up for Hickstead, but that was all he needed.

Gary Parsonage riding Peter Street to victory in the 2009 Eventing Grand Prix. This win brought Gary level with Pippa Funnell and her record of three wins in this class: he also won in 1999 and 2008.

HICKSTEAD

The National Schools and Pony Club Jumping Championships

'Equestrianism helps young people to grow in personal confidence, act responsibly, identify and address challenges, and equips them to assess and manage risk.' — TIM MANLY

As well as aiming to attract the world's top internationals, Hickstead has, from the beginning, also nurtured younger riders. Douglas Bunn started junior competitions in 1962, and said that they 'transformed the place. Not only did children turn up in droves, but so did their parents, and other relatives came as well'. So he was very receptive when the late Peter Booth, Archdeacon of Lewes, suggested that the showground should host an annual inter-school championship.

The first National Schools Jumping Championships were held in 1964, and two years later the Pony Club Jumping Championships were added. They have been held every August since then, except in 1986 when the whole meeting had to be cancelled because of torrential rain. In recent years the championships have been sponsored by Hurstpierpoint College, just a few miles from Hickstead and with which the Bunn family has built up a close relationship.

The late Canon Peter Booth.

Although only nine schools entered the inaugural championships, Lillesden winning the senior title and Ashford the junior, the chance of being able to ride in Hickstead's famed International Arena proved an irresistible bait, and 12 months later the number had risen to 27.

These days there are regularly more than 100 teams competing from all parts of the British Isles and Ireland, with occasional overseas visitors. The latter have had their successes, too, with St David's School in Johannesburg winning the senior championship in 1973 and the New English School, Kuwait, following suit 10 years later. The schools teams are made up of three riders each and the Pony Club teams of four riders. Individual awards for all three categories were started in 2004.

Qualifying rounds are held in the outside rings, with some eight to 10 teams winning through to each of the finals, which are staged in the International Arena. Although there is no prize-money, the competition to gain one of the medals that go to the placed horses, and the Hickstead Sashes awarded to the winners, is every bit as intense as for the valuable international classes.

In 2009 the senior championships alone attracted no fewer than 67 teams and resulted in a triumph for the enterprising trio from Cowbridge Comprehensive School in Glamorgan. Instead of relying on adults to do it for them, the three riders, Louise Edwards with Myrddin, Josh Rees, who rode Silver Sunburst, and Bethan Allman on Murvey McCoy, persuaded local businesses to sponsor them.

They justified this support by winning—beating Stonar School, who have the best record of all in these championships. Stonar won the senior title in 1991, 2004, 2006 and 2007, and the junior in 1992-94 and again in 1996, as well as providing the 2009 individual champion in Sarah Pinfield on Samba.

Since Loreto College triumphed in 1997, Irish teams have been regularly among the winners, with Kilkenny College taking both senior and junior team titles in 2005. They shared third place with Mayfield in 2009, were beaten only by Backwell Comprehensive, from Bristol, Avon, in a jump-off in 2008 and produced the individual senior champion of 2009 in Luke Cummins on Rathurtin.

Pinewood School from Shrivenham, Wiltshire, fielded the 2009 junior winning team. Fransiska Goess Sarau on Daisy, Caitlin Belsham on Bobby Sox and Jessica Mendoza (the individual junior champion in 2007 and 2008) with Dooneens Future Star, finished ahead

PAGE 144: Mr Tim Manly, headmaster of Hurstpierpoint College, presents the awards to the individual junior champion 2009, Sarah Pinfield from Stonar School.

of Millfield A and Stonar.

Since the Belvoir won the first Pony Club Championship in 1966, the title has gone to just about every part of the country, and across the Irish Sea. No team has had a monopoly of success, but the Iveagh from Country Armagh had an unbeaten run from 2002-05, and in 2004 and 2005 also provided the individual champions in Claire Percy and Declan McParland.

In 2009 the Iveagh finished equal fourth, but Amanda Hylands won the individual championship for them on Picanto, with the team title going for the first time to the Fitzwilliam quartet of Georgie Armstrong on Golden Class, Jenny Martell on Bounce, Emily Meredith on Pudding and Georgie Fenn on Rosie.

Not surprisingly, Hurstpierpoint College are keen participants in the Schools Championships, and in 2008 Ellie Brown, Douglas Bunn's granddaughter, whose mother Lizzie is Hickstead's show secretary as well as being a director, helped them take the junior silver medal behind Queen Margaret's School, represented by Daisy Miller, Rosanna Lambert and Sophie Beatty, who had journeyed down from York.

Ellie was riding Baskin Bay, owned by her uncle Shane Breen, Chloe's husband who is himself a consistent winner at Hickstead and elsewhere, while also in the team were Amy Inglis, the daughter of Duncan, another regular in Hickstead's international competitions who also rode in the Schools Championships, on her father's J's Junior and Benjy Mason on his own Mango.

Familiar names in the main arena have regularly appeared in the Schools Championships. One of these, Robert Whitaker, whose family has played such an important part in Hickstead's 50-year history, has said, perhaps a little tongue-in-cheek: 'If it wasn't for the Schools and Pony Clubs I wouldn't have got nearly as much practice in the main ring!'

The Duchess of York, as Sarah Ferguson; supermodel Jodie Kidd, Douglas Bunn's god-daughter; and Clare Balding, the BBC's outstanding equestrian and racing presenter, are others who had an early experience of show jumping at the Schools Championships.

Tim Manly, headmaster of Hurstpierpoint College, is a firm believer in the benefits of sport in general and riding especially. He said: 'Equestrianism helps young people to grow in personal confidence, act responsibly, identify and address challenges—both as solo and team performers—and equips them to assess and manage risk'. In an era when any sort of risk-taking is increasingly curtailed by officialdom, the Schools and Pony Club Championships clearly have a rôle that goes beyond sport.

ABOVE: Lizzie Bunn's daughter, Ellie Brown, and Baskin Bay, who helped Hurstpierpoint College finish second in the 2008 National Junior Team Championship

'Astonishing'

Dressage at Hickstead

by Jane Kidd

'Douglas's foresight in including dressage at Hickstead has elevated the sport in Great Britain to the highest level, and provided a venue that now rivals the top European shows.' — DANE RAWLINS

Douglas Bunn created Hickstead according to continental principles. He wanted to provide British competitors with the same up-to-date facilities that were available across the Channel. This inevitably led to including dressage as well as show jumping, as almost all the big European shows run the two disciplines side by side.

The early history of dressage at Hickstead was a stop-start one, and it took the resilience and determination of Dane Rawlins to put it there firmly on the map. Thanks to him and his team, leading riders from all over the world are now keen to compete in these top class facilities. Major championships have been staged and the British public have been able to see high level events on home soil. In 2009 Edward Gal and Moorlands Totilas scored a world record 89.5% in the Kür there. They have since raised the bar even higher.

To a large extent, Dane has achieved his aim: 'I had spent so much time abroad and wanted to bring some of what they had to England. To get that type of show here was the way forward for the sport.'

THE BRITISH DRESSAGE DERBY

Douglas had modelled his show-jumping course on that of Hamburg, where they ran the famous Derby; but they also had one for dressage riders. The Hamburg Dressage Derby was a very special test for the riders, as only four combinations qualified for a final and in this they rode each other's horses. Points were added to determine a winning rider and a winning horse. This testing form of competition was what Douglas introduced to Hickstead.

The aircraft runway, being flat, was chosen as the site, and through special contacts the 1948 Olympic arena boards were obtained (actually they were illegal as they were so high, but they were much more decorative than modern equivalents). Great trophies were awarded and the best in Britain took part: Jook Hall, Lorna Johnstone, Domini Morgan and Jennie Loriston-Clarke among them. For the 24-year-old David Hunt this was his first major competition and he commented: 'It had an exciting international atmosphere that was very different from any other show in England.'

The Hickstead Dressage Derby grew in stature and in 1973 a German contingent was lured across the Channel. Herbert Rehbein, one of the greatest rider/trainers of the 20th century, took the title of British Dressage Derby winner, and when I visited him shortly before his death he proudly showed me the trophy he had won nearly three decades before.

In Britain the show jumping and dressage cultures are very different, and at this meeting there was a clash which ended in the dressage group (the forerunner of British Dressage) refusing to sanction further dressage at Hickstead.

A NEW START

A few years later, as a new recruit to dressage, I was delighted when Douglas agreed to my running some dressage shows, and pretty disturbed when I was not allowed to do so by the dressage authorities. After some negotiating, low-level competitions were permitted, and each year we were allowed to step up the grades to run the British Dressage Derby again, this time as an accumulator on points won in the small tour classes.

As before, the arenas were laid out on the runway and, whenever possible, watered. However there were handicaps other than the grass surface. Hackney ponies and their carriages prepared for their show in the international arena alongside the dressage arenas. This terrified many of the dressage horses, as did some of the helicopters that landed near by.

One loose cavalry horse actually jumped in and out of that 1948 Olympic arena, but fortunately the rider competing at the time was a horseman, kept his horse focussed, and the test was completed without any blips. This was not the rarefied dressage for which Britain was recognised during the 1970s. It was, however, prestigious and fun, with prize-

givings in the main arena and some victory rounds at a gallop.

There were, too, different sorts of competitions. Douglas promoted the thoroughbred by presenting a trophy for the most successful one at the show, and there were combined training competitions, for which most of the top eventers competed. Princess Anne won it twice, on her European Champion Doublet and on her Olympic horse Goodwill.

However, when the most popular facilities in the world, at Goodwood, became free for national competitions I moved on to help the Duchess of Richmond run them, and nobody else volunteered to run dressage at Hickstead.

DANE TAKES OVER

In 1989 Dane Rawlins took six horses for a dressage display in Hickstead's Main Arena, and afterwards asked Douglas: 'When are you going to have dressage back at Hickstead?' Dane remembers that Douglas's reply was: 'If you want dressage here you will bloody well have to do it yourself. But it must be a CDIO (an official international).' It was in 1993, four years later, that dressage was re-established at Hickstead.

Dane Rawlins was not going to make do with grass arenas but wanted to establish as good a reputation as that enjoyed by the neighbouring show-jumping facilities. His aim was to provide facilities that were comparable with those in Europe.

In negotiations with Douglas he was allotted land that was entirely separate from the show jumping. Here he had the scope to develop the facilities he wanted, but nothing could be started until funds were raised. He needed two full-size arenas (today there are four), proper judges' boxes (today they are as good as any in the world), safe, spacious stables, and, most importantly, people to help. And, said Dane: 'I had a team of dressage nuts, and they are almost all still here.'

Dane said: 'I asked David Crockford to help, and the late Paul Milham, who got people together and did the funding. My wife Maureen and Marie Mepham, who is now the dressage show secretary, were also part of the team, and John Millis, who is brilliant with electronics. Hickstead was the first show in the world to have electronic judges' marks. We had some problems with the FEI about this, but the next year Aachen had them, and now almost all the big shows do.'

While the plans were being made, Goodwood (regular winner of the award for the best dressage show in the world) was flourishing. Dane said: 'I knew we could only be second

Lorna Johnson and El Guapo being presented with their trophy after winning the 1968 British Dressage Derby

Laura Bechtolsheimer in celebratory mood.

fiddle to Goodwood, but I talked to the Duchess of Richmond, and as the two sites were close I hoped riders might stay over if we ran the shows consecutively.'

But during the four years it took to get the project off the ground, Goodwood had replaced dressage horses with fast cars. Hickstead was going to be Britain's most important dressage international.

HELPING THE YOUNG

From the start, Dane was determined to give the young plenty of opportunities at this international. He had been instrumental in starting BYRDS (British Young Riders Dressage Scheme), had trained many young riders, and acted as chef d'équipe to Under 21s teams. The development of the dressage youth was an important project for him. Consequently Hickstead ran numerous young rider, junior and pony rider national and international shows alongside the senior internationals. The young have been given many opportunities in competitions, displays and as helpers. The first official championships to be awarded to Hickstead were for Juniors and Young Riders in 1998 and it was a big boost that not only did they run smoothly and were popular with competitors but the British junior team won their first medal, a bronze, at a European Championships.

THE YOUNG HORSES

It has not been just the young riders but also the young horses for which great opportunities have been provided. From the start, Dressage at Hickstead took over the Pet Plan Young Horse Championships for five- and six-year-old horses that had begun at Addington. They have continued to champion the classes that identify future stars, to give the inexperienced the chance to compete in inspiring conditions and for assessments to be made by world-famous trainers and riders.

LOOKING AFTER THE AMATEURS

Nor have the grass-roots riders been neglected at Hickstead: there have been plenty of unaffiliated shows and the whole spectrum of grades from preliminary through to Grand Prix are usually part of the Hickstead international week. A Masters series, with each grade being given qualifying competitions and a final during this international week, has enabled many amateurs to get a taste of a highly-charged atmosphere and to warm up alongside top riders.

THE EUROPEAN CHAMPIONSHIPS

To date, Dressage at Hickstead's greatest achievement was the staging of the 2003 European Championships. They drew capacity crowds who created a most vibrant atmosphere. There were standing ovations for the great tests and plenty of clapping and cheers for each and every competitor. It gave a new perspective to dressage. The sport that was so often dismissed as 'like watching paint dry' came of age and became a spectator sport. The weather and the background music that matched the hoof beats of the horses all helped, and the success of the British team—veterans Richard Davison on Ballaseyr Royale and Emile Faurie with Rascher Hopes, and newcomers Emma Hindle on Wie Weltmeyer and Nicola McGivern with Active Walero—who took a bronze medal, certainly added plenty of excitement. But it was the organisation that was the key element. These European Championships at Hickstead set new levels of excellence in terms of entertainment and efficiency.

Germany predictably won the team gold, and Ulla Salzgeber on Rusty the individual. Veteran team manager Ferdi Wassermeyer told Dane that it was the best show he had ever been to. The special feature was that it was a show run by the riders for the riders. Among the 70-odd volunteers who made the show happen, the majority were riders. It cost just short of a million pounds to stage and that is what is holding Dane back from doing it again.

Emma Hindle and Wie Weltmeyer, who made their championship debut in the team that earned Britain a bronze medal in the 2003 European Championships at Hickstead

The Berkeley Group plc
HOLLEY
GRANGE HOTELS
LONDON
H'F PASSES 7 7 7 7 7

AN OVERVIEW

Looking back over the years of Dressage at Hickstead Dane said: 'I have not achieved as much as I wanted to. The most enjoyable events were the Young Rider Europeans and the Senior Europeans. I would like Hickstead to be more popular, but to achieve this we need finance. We have a good steering committee and they keep coming up with ideas.'

For Dane the highlights have been: 'Watching the Brits win that bronze medal in 2003. Seeing my riders coming through and getting their pocket badge for riding for Britain. Hickstead has brought on the less experienced. I am especially pleased with the Hickstead Dressage Masters. Every county in Great Britain holds a qualifying round and there are others in Ireland, north and south, and the Channel Islands, and we hold the final during the Royal International.'

It is not just the competitions for which Hickstead is famous. The parties are all-night affairs and the show-jumping lines are pretty deserted on the evenings the dressage people have their parties. Dane remembers: 'The *It's a Knockout* hosted by Noel Edmunds at the 2003 European Championships stands out for me.'

There used to be a grand ball but it has been trimmed down into a popular gala evening. At this there is plenty of entertainment, and a feature is the opportunity for show jumpers and eventers to show off their dressage prowess in a novel challenge. They jump fences and in between them do dressage movements. This is an event which epitomises Dane's liking for innovation and a good sense of fun. It also provides a dimension that he supports: 'To bring the sports closer together.'

THE SUPPORT TEAM

Dane is well aware of the importance of helpers: 'It is the team effort that makes it work. There are so many and they are a bright bunch that come up with ideas and stop me from adopting some of my crazier ideas.' His wife Maureen, a very intelligent financial highflyer, will turn her hand to anything and everything when it comes to the show days. Marie Mepham has worked for Dane since 1991 and has been the show secretary since 2004. Look down the list of officials on the show programmes and one sees that many have been there for years. Dane might disturb the establishment, upset many with his single-minded determination to achieve a point, but he keeps his followers.

The late Douglas Bunn and he had much in common—vision, the confidence to obtain their goals and the ability to ignore those who say 'no' or 'it cannot be done'. This is what it has taken to make Dressage at Hickstead work.

Dressage at Hickstead founder, Dane Rawlins, listens to yet more advice from 'The Master'! Douglas's eldest daughter, Claudia, looks on.

OPPOSITE PAGE: The Hickstead International Dressage Arena during the 2003 European Dressage Championship

SOUTH AFRICA
2
SOUTH AFRICA
3
3
Audi
25

Polo at Hickstead

'Hickstead has created one of the most modern and impressive arenas in the country. Not only has it hosted very successful international matches but it has worked hard to encourage the young to play.'

— NICHOLAS J.A. COLQUHOUN-DENVERS, CHAIRMAN HPA

Most of the sport at Hickstead may happen during the summer months, but since June 2006, and under the direction of John Bunn, polo has added a new dimension to the All England Jumping Course's increasingly diverse activities through the winter.

Arena polo, which has been played in England for more than 20 years, is to the summer game what rugby sevens or five-a-side football are to their traditional sports: though on a smaller scale, with three in a team instead of four, a larger, softer ball and shorter chukkas, it is every bit as hectic and exciting as its bigger cousin.

John Bunn and Jack Kidd, one of three resident HPA coaches at the Sussex showground, have been friends since childhood and, both obsessed with polo, dreamed of bringing it to Hickstead. When a new warm-up arena for the national jumping classes was needed for the improvement of the summer shows, the pair of them cunningly convinced Douglas to have it built to the perfect dimensions for an arena polo pitch. It took little thereafter to convert it into a state-of-the-art, fully-boarded 100m by 50m arena, now complete with viewing area and a well-used clubhouse.

Daisy Bunn, Hickstead's sponsorship director, remembers: 'Following in Dad's footsteps we concentrated on securing sponsorship so we could provide the best experience possible, for competitors and spectators. In my first week full-time in the office I stupidly offered to help with running the polo, believing I could squeeze in a few hours here and there. I soon realised this was no part-time job, as after just one season we had more playing members than any other winter club in the UK. At the beginning we had the same reaction as Dad did when he first opened the gates: "who does this cocky upstart think he is, calling his new place the All England Jumping Course." People were not convinced when we opened the All England Polo Club, but they soon were, and we have enjoyed incredible support from competitors, spectators and the powers-that-be.'

Jack Kidd, a former European and World gold medallist, is among the third generation of a family which has been associated with Hickstead from its earliest days. His grandmother, the Hon. Janet Kidd, won the British Driving Derby in 1974 and was a long-serving director; his father John, also a polo international, and aunt Jane, were frequently in the winner's enclosure after jumping competitions, and Jane also ran the dressage at Hickstead for a while.

Games at all levels, from weekly club chukkas up to internationals, are played there during a season which lasts from November to March, and in January 2008 included the first ever Arena Polo Test Match, between England and South Africa. Hickstead already had a strong relationship with television broadcasters through their show-jumping competitions, and so were able to get coverage of it on Sky Sports. In February 2010, in conjunction with the HPA, the sport's governing body, they staged their third international test match which, at 24 goals, was the highest calibre ever played in arena polo in Britain.

Nicholas J.A. Colquhoun-Denvers, chairman of the HPA, is very supportive. He said: 'Hickstead has always been synonymous with equestrianism at the highest level, and the Hurlingham Polo Association is delighted that it has branched out into arena polo and created one of the most modern and impressive arenas in the country. Not only has it hosted very successful international matches which have had a real impact on arena polo at the highest level, but it has worked hard to encourage the young to play, and provided a wonderful opportunity for people to enjoy polo all the year round'.

As with all aspects of equestrian sport at Hickstead, be it jumping, dressage and now polo, the younger generation are also supported and encouraged, with training and competitions for schools and pony riders.

PAGE 156: Hickstead staged the first ever Arena Polo Test Match, in 2008, between South Africa and England.

TOP (RIGHT TO LEFT): Girls Aloud's Sarah Harding playing at the Club in 2007; Matt Pannell watches as Sarah Wiseman stretches for a long shot; Club director John Bunn is a keen umpire as well as regular polo player.

BOTTOM (LEFT TO RIGHT): Tim Bown 'rides off' Jack Kidd at speed; In a celebratory mood (from left to right): Brad Shackleton, Kevin Shaw, Seb Baker and Chris Warren;

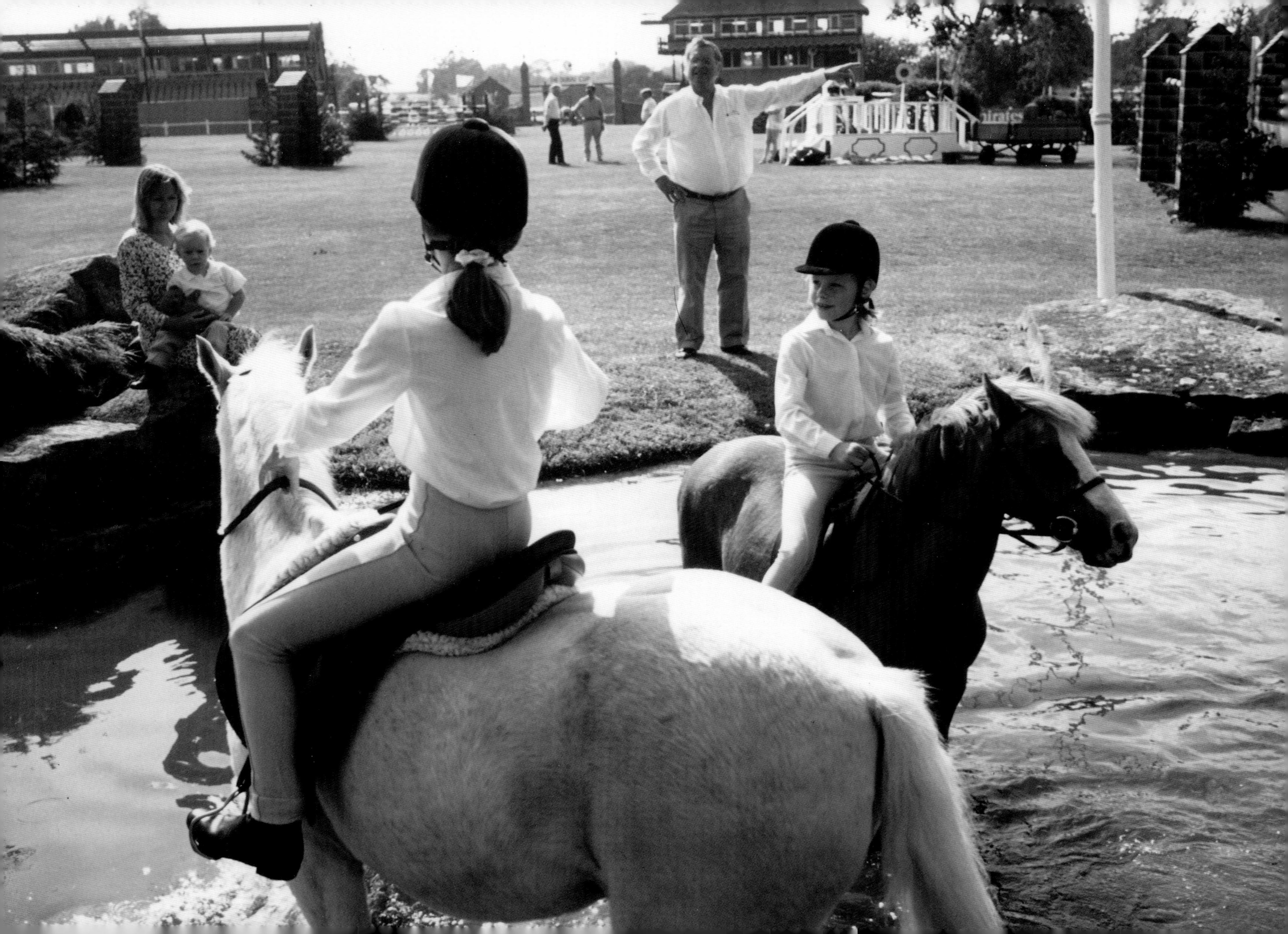

The Family and the Future

'Dad put millions into Hickstead because he was passionate about horses, and show jumping in particular. Now his financial input is gone we have to find ways to continue his legacy into the future.' – LIZZIE BUNN

Douglas Bunn was always the driving force at Hickstead—not for nothing was he known as 'The Master of Hickstead'—but he knew how to delegate. Much of that delegation fell on the shoulders of six of his nine surviving children: Edward, Lizzie, John, Chloe, Daisy and Charlie. They grew up with the showground as their playground as well as their home, and as youngsters had to earn their pocket money by working on the most routine of tasks, from washing and painting the jumps before the show, to clearing up the rubbish afterwards, at 50p per bag. When Daisy added to her collection a mound of bags that had already been filled by some of the tidier exhibitors, Douglas, who watched her do it, paid her anyway. He always encouraged enterprise.

Edward and Lizzie have been more or less running the show for some 15 years, with a well-established division of labour: Lizzie, who took over as Organising Secretary in 1987 from Anita Arnett—who had done the job for 18 years but retired to travel the show circuit with legendary Australian rider Kevin Bacon—is in charge in the office, and Edward oversees all that goes on outside.

Lizzie said: 'With Dad we made up a three-man team. We could always go to him for advice, and if someone suggested something that we did not want to happen, we could say that "Dad wouldn't like it!"' She had a great working relationship with her father, and was with him when in 1991 he had to decide whether to take on the Royal International Horse Show: 'We went to Belgrave Square for a meeting about it, and were met at the door by Peter Fenwick, the chairman of the organising committee, who told us the main sponsor had withdrawn. We went into a room on our own and Dad asked what I thought we should do. He had always wanted to host the show so I said he should go for it. And he did, a brave decision he never regretted.'

Edward, after studying at the Royal Agricultural College, went to work on a cotton farm in Australia. He said: 'My Dad wanted me home, so we came to an agreement that I would if I could become the showground manager. I started working full time in May 1983, and 27 seasons later I am still here. In 1986 I married my wife Julia and we live with our four children, Tom, Lucy, William and Oliver, in a house in the grounds. Lucy is the horsey one—she rides up to 10 horses a day for Shane and Chloe. Julia and I, as very hands-on heads of the logistics team for Breen Equestrian, regularly drive Shane's horseboxes in convoy to shows on the Continent. Without Julia, none of what I have done would have been possible.'

Edward, who has juggled his Hickstead duties with being a part-time fireman since 1992 and is now Station Commander at Hurstpierpoint—'It gives me a lot of pleasure, and is my bit for the community'—is responsible for the upkeep of all the buildings and facilities, and, crucially, for the arenas, and the jumping surfaces: 'Our biggest challenge is the British weather. When it is dry, there is no finer ground, but these days we get more extremes. There is a school of thought that we should put an all-weather surface into the International Arena, but there is no way that is going to happen. With modern technology and soil science there are ways of creating a turf arena that will cope. It has been done in Dublin and hopefully by 2011 we will have an arena that looks the same as now but rides well whatever the weather throws at it. Once the groundwork has been completed we should be in a position to tender for future championships.'

Lizzie started working in the office, in 1983: 'Putting into practice what I learned at secretarial college. In those days we had manual typewriters and an old-fashioned Gestetner machine for copying. The changes in communication have been massive, and when my office staff complain about their computers crashing or not being able to read a fax, I tell them how we had to write all the entries by hand with a piece of carbon paper, and sent telegrams if we had to contact someone urgently. On-line entries, credit card advance sales and data-capturing via our website were inconceivable back then.

PAGE 160: Douglas Bunn tries to get his young daughters Chloe and Daisy to leave the Hickstead lake. His third wife, Lorna (with their son, Charlie) looks on.

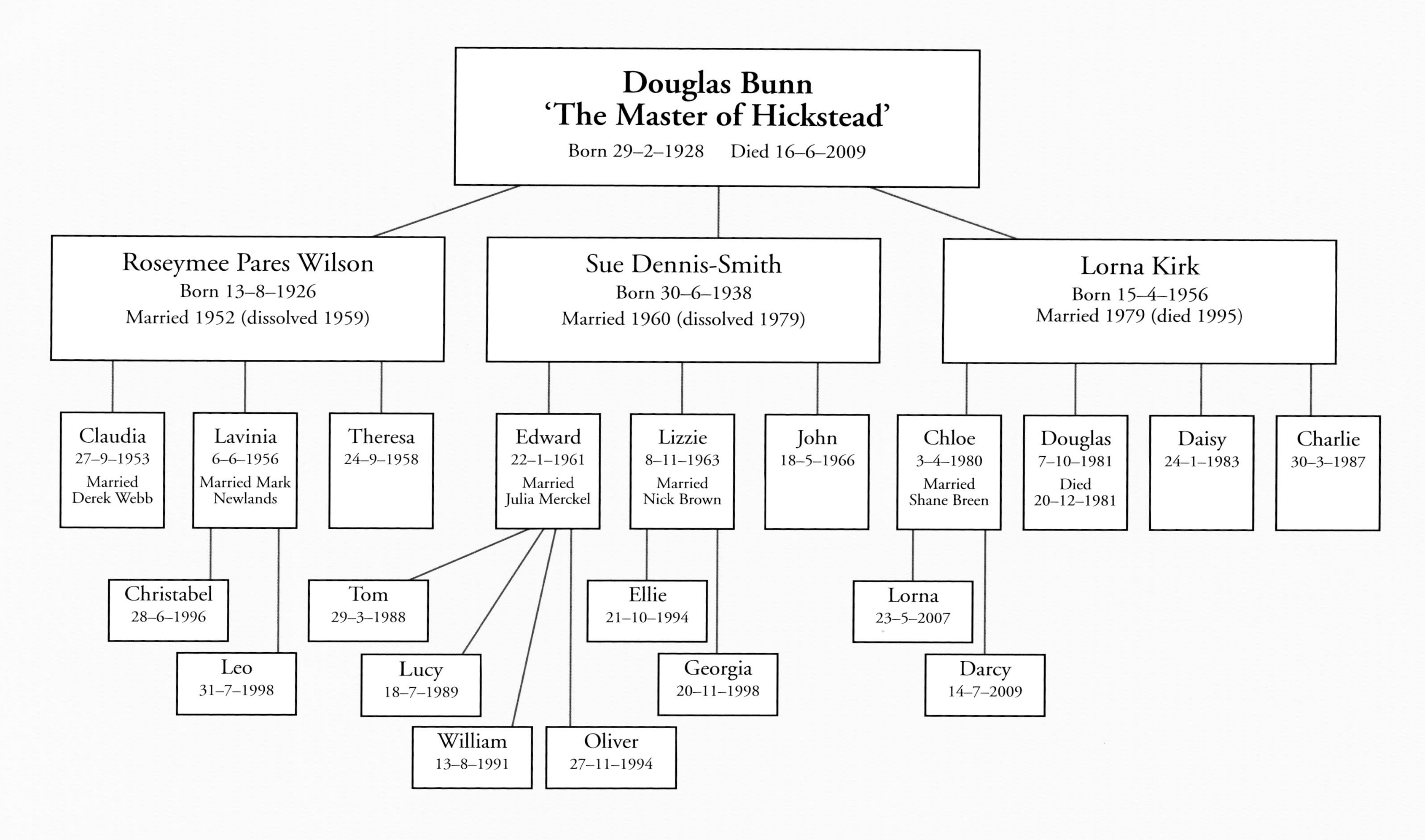

Douglas Bunn
'The Master of Hickstead'
Born 29–2–1928 Died 16–6–2009
Roseymee Pares Wilson
Born 13–8–1926
Married 1952 (dissolved 1959)
Sue Dennis-Smith
Born 30–6–1938
Married 1960 (dissolved 1979)
Lorna Kirk
Born 15–4–1956
Married 1979 (died 1995)
Claudia
27–9–1953
Married Derek Webb
Lavinia
6–6–1956
Married Mark Newlands
Theresa
24–9–1958
Edward
22–1–1961
Married Julia Merckel
Lizzie
8–11–1963
Married Nick Brown
John
18–5–1966
Chloe
3–4–1980
Married Shane Breen
Douglas
7–10–1981
Died 20–12–1981
Daisy
24–1–1983
Charlie
30–3–1987
Christabel
28–6–1996
Leo
31–7–1998
Tom
29–3–1988
Lucy
18–7–1989
William
13–8–1991
Oliver
27–11–1994
Ellie
21–10–1994
Georgia
20–11–1998
Lorna
23–5–2007
Darcy
14–7–2009

'I have been extremely lucky over the years to work with a number of extraordinary individuals, both permanent staff and show regulars. Their loyal and unstinting support, come rain or shine and often with little or no reward, has made a huge contribution to Hickstead's success.

'Many people think we shut down over the winter and re-open a few weeks before the first show. In fact, keeping Hickstead going is a full-time job—a bit like painting the Forth Bridge. As soon as one season ends, we start planning for the next one.

'Dad put millions into Hickstead because he was passionate about horses, and show jumping in particular. Now his financial input is gone we have to find ways to continue his legacy into the future, and make the showground economically secure. In recent years we have had to diversify and now have a full and varied calendar of corporate and social events, conferences, concerts—we even have a licence for weddings! It is my dream that the showground will continue to flourish so that in a few years time my daughters, Georgia and Ellie, and the next generation, can take over the reins.'

A Bunn family gathering: (left to right) Charlie, Chloe, Claudia, Daisy, Lavinia, John, Douglas, Lizzie and Edward

John, the third of Douglas's children with Sue, who still lives in a house in the grounds and has a permanent box at the shows, took a different, but no less important, path. He said: 'If we wanted pocket money we had to work during our school holidays, mowing the grass or painting fences. This approach taught me the value of money from an early age, and also taught me I could not work under the direct daily gaze of my father. It was as a result of this that I took over the caravan holiday business in Selsey which Dad started in 1959 that has proved the backbone of the family business over the years.'

His position has remained principally a financial one, but when, aged 23, a knee injury put an end to his rugby playing (for Harrow and later for Sussex and Harlequins), he turned with equal enthusiasm to polo. And in 2006 he and Jack Kidd, whose family has been involved with Hickstead since it began, introduced arena polo to Hickstead's ever-expanding schedule of events, a venture that has quickly proved an outstanding success.

Douglas's three surviving children with his late wife Lorna have come into the business later—Chloe and Daisy both having outside interests—but their enthusiasm

> *'Douglas was one of life's great characters; he was larger than life, a very generous man, and above all a wonderful father to his nine surviving children. Along with Hickstead they are his legacy and are all a credit to this very special and unique man who will be greatly missed. The six youngest will ensure that Hickstead will continue to be a centre of excellence.'*
>
> CAROLA GODMAN LAW

is no less for that. Chloe followed her father both into studying law and riding successfully, though her initial attempts were less glorious: 'In my very first class at Hickstead, on an 11.2hh pony, I was eliminated at the first fence. Things improved after that, but on my first time in the main ring, on a 13.2 pony, again I was again eliminated at the first. Dad was not amused!'

Chloe more than made up for this, however, by giving Douglas one of his proudest ever moments when she won the Speed Derby on Citi Dancer in 1999.

'Despite not being on the Hickstead payroll, as this is the ultimate family business, my whole life revolves around Hickstead. My siblings always considered it rather helpful to have a rider "on the circuit" to lend a valuable rider's view to the running of it. This rôle has been enthusiastically taken up by my husband, Shane, while I have been on maternity leave, looking after my daughters Lorna and Darcy.'

Daisy spent five years in the office, learning the ropes from Lizzie, before going to Edinburgh University to read English Literature and Russian. Now she combines running her own photography business in London with being Hickstead's Sponsorship Director. She said: 'Although I only work part-time at Hickstead I take it very seriously. Dad was a master innovator and it was his constant encouragement to think creatively and move with the times that has helped me understand the unique needs of sponsors and the commercial possibilities open to Hickstead. The future, and the inevitable changes it will bring, is a daunting prospect, but I believe that in the motley crew Dad has taught and entrusted to take the business on, we possess such a wide variety of skills and interests, and above all a shared sense of steely determination, that we will succeed, no matter what.'

Charlie, the youngest of the six and an actor, has in recent years presided as host in his father's box at the show, helping look after the sponsors, guests, stewards and judges, and making sure they realise how much they are appreciated: 'This was a job in which I couldn't have survived without George Rottner, front of house in Dad's box and one of the people who I feel gives Hickstead the wonderful atmosphere that so many people enjoy. Edward and Lizzie are already doing a great job running things, and having Breen Equestrian at Hickstead is a huge asset—Shane and Chloe make a fantastic team. When I think of the future of Hickstead I get an enormous feeling of excitement for the challenges that lie ahead of us as a family.'

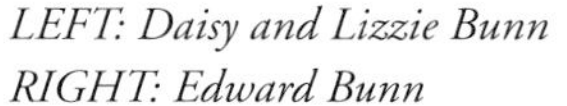

LEFT: Daisy and Lizzie Bunn
RIGHT: Edward Bunn

Index

The main arena at the All England Jumping Course at Hickstead in the mid-sixties.

...and as it is today, with permanent seating for over 5,000 spectators and 26 corporate hospitality suites.

Bibliography and Credits

BIBLIOGRAPHY

Ammann, Max E. *FEI Championships*, Fédération Equestre Internationale, 2007
Broome, David, with Genevieve Murphy. *Jump-Off,* Stanley Paul, 1971
Clarke, Sue. *'Forgie', the story of Pennwood Forge Mill*, Quartilles International, 1979
Clayton, Michael & Tracey, Dick. *Hickstead, the First Twelve Years*, Pelham Books, 1972
Coakes, Marion. *Book of Horses*, Pelham Books, 1968
Draper, Judith. *Guinness Show Jumping, Records, Facts & Champions.* Guinness Superlatives, 1987
Draper, Judith. *The Stars of Show Jumping*, Stanley Paul, 1990
Macgregor-Morris, Pamela & Smith, Alan. *Horse & Rider Yearbooks*, 1974-1980, Queen Anne Press
Slavin, Michael. *Show Jumping Legends*, Ireland 1868-1998, Wolfhound Press, 1998

PICTURE CREDITS

The publishers would like to thank the following people and photographic libraries for permission to reproduce their material. Every care has been taken to trace the copyright holders. However, if we have omitted anyone we apologise, and will, if informed, make corrections in any future edition.

Key: **t** top; **b** bottom; **c** centre; **l** left; **r** right

BBC 83; **Jean Bridel** 19, 25, 74; **Budd** 41, 43, 45; **Lizzie Bunn** 16; **John Connor Associates** front jacket r; **Erin Cowgill** 122; **Findlay Davidson** 20l; **Srdja Dukanovic** 8, 20r; **FEI Leslie Lane** 26, 30, 31, 33l, 33tr, 33br, 34l, 34r, 35l, 35r, 36, 47, 48, 51, 52, 69, 81; **FEI/Werner Ernst** 54, 55; **Caroline Finch** 148; **Fiona Forbes** 11; **Nigel Goddard** 5l; **Clive Hiles** 109, 133tl, 141br; **Horse & Hound/Syndication** front jacket l, front jacket c, 2, 4lc, 4c, 4rc, 4r, 5lc, 57, 58, 59, 66, 73tl, 73bcl, 77, 78r, 86, 89, 90, 93, 94, 97, 101, 102, 104l, 104r, 110, 113r, 114, 117, 118, 121, 128,129, 130, 133tc, 133br, 134tl, 134tr, 134bc, 134br, 136, 137, 138, 142, 143, 152, 153, 154, 165r; **Horse & Rider** 28, 63t; **Samantha Lamb** 5r, 73tr, 73bcr, 124, 141l; **Leslie Lane** 24, 38, 60, 63b, 70, 133tr, 134bl, 141tr, 151, 166; **Ross Laney** 84; **Silvio Mariani** 64; **Roy Maton** 167; **Trevor Meeks/Horse & Hound** 23, 106, 113l, 132; **Ian Michaelwaite** 5c, 156, 159tl, 159tc, 159bl; **Newsquest** 4l, 15, 53; **Craig Payne** 73bl, 73br; **John Periam** 159br; **Julian Portch** 127; **Pleasure Prints** 5rc, 133bl, 133bc, 144, 147, 165l; **PA-Peuter** 42; **PA** 6; **Tony Ramirez** 159tr, 159bc; **Ramsey & Muspratt Archive, Cambridgeshire Collection, Cambridge Central Library** 14; **Shoreham College** 146; **Kevin Sparrow** 155; **Studio Graphic** 78; **Helen Tinner Photography** 164; **WD & HO Wills** 103

First published in 2010 by Hickstead Publishing
The All England Jumping Course
Hickstead
West Sussex
RH17 5NU

www.hickstead.co.uk

Design and Production: Paul Harding
Publishing Consultant: Barbara Cooper

Colour reproduction by Typongraph Digital Systems, Italy
Printed in China by Eurasia

5 4 3 2 1

ISBN: 978-0-9565231-0-5

A Cataloguing-in-Publication record for this book is available from the British Library.